DEALING WITH
DIFFERENCES
IN MARRIAGE

DEALING WITH
DIFFERENCES
IN MARRIAGE

BRENT A. BARLOW

Deseret Book Company
Salt Lake City, Utah

"Identity Crisis," by Gloria Rosenthal, reprinted by permission of Cartoon Features Syndicate.

Excerpt, page 13, from Frank Cox, *Human Intimacy: Marriage, the Family and Its Meaning*, 5th ed. (St. Paul, Minnesota: West Publishing Company, 1987), reprinted by permission.

Excerpts, pages 29–31, from *What Every Woman Should Know about Men* by Dr. Joyce Brothers. Reprinted by permission of Harold Ober Associates Incorporated. Copyright © 1981 by Joyce B. Enterprises, Inc.

List, pages 69–70, excerpted from the book *Incompatibility: Grounds for a Great Marriage* by Chuck and Barb Snyder, published by Questar Publishers, Inc., ©1988 Chuck and Barb Snyder, reprinted by permission.

Library of Congress Cataloging-in-Publication Data

Barlow, Brent A., 1941–
    Dealing with differences in marriage / Brent A. Barlow.
        p.   cm.
    Includes bibliographical references and index.
    ISBN 0–87579–732–6
       1. Marriage.   2. Marriage—Religious aspects—Mormon Church.
I. Title.
BX8641.B28   1993
248.8'44—dc20   93–11070
                                                   CIP

Printed in the United States of America

10   9   8   7   6   5   4   3   2   1

IDENTITY CRISIS

There are two types of people (so say the reports):
One loves opera; the other loves sports;
One loves the mountains; the other, the ocean;
One wants to relax; the other craves motion;
One prefers silence each morning—no matter!
The other one thrives on a morning of chatter:
And what causes them so much struggle and strife?
They always end up . . . as husband and wife!

Gloria Rosenthal
The Wall Street Journal Book of Wit

CONTENTS

ACKNOWLEDGMENTS   ix

PART 1
DIFFERENCES AND THEIR EFFECTS
ON MARRIAGE   1

CHAPTER 1
INTRODUCTION   3

CHAPTER 2
THE IMPORTANCE OF DIFFERENCES   8

CHAPTER 3
UNATTENDED DIFFERENCES:
THE PATHWAY TO DIVORCE   16

CHAPTER 4
SOURCES OF DIFFERENCES   25

CHAPTER 5
SEXUAL DIFFERENCES IN MARRIAGE   39

CHAPTER 6
BRENT AND SUSAN'S DIFFERENCES   57

PART 2
WAYS TO DEAL WITH DIFFERENCES
IN MARRIAGE   67

CHAPTER 7
IDENTIFYING YOUR DIFFERENCES   69

CHAPTER 8
THE CHANGE-FIRST PRINCIPLE   75

CHAPTER 9
THE TEN Cs: THE FOUNDATION OF COMMITMENT,
CARING, AND COMMUNICATION   85

CHAPTER 10
THE TEN Cs: THE FREQUENT FOUR OF COEXISTENCE,
CAPITULATION, COMPROMISE, AND COLLABORATION   96

CHAPTER 11
THE TEN Cs: THE SPECIAL CIRCUMSTANCES OF
CONFRONTATION AND COUNSELING   108

CHAPTER 12
THE TEN Cs: THE TREMENDOUS POWER OF CHRIST   120

PART 3
WAYS OF VIEWING DIFFERENCES
IN MARRIAGE   133

CHAPTER 13
NEW PERSPECTIVES ON DIFFERENCES   135

CHAPTER 14
CASE STUDIES   143

NOTES   151

INDEX   157

ACKNOWLEDGMENTS

I am indebted to the many who assisted in the production of *Dealing with Differences in Marriage.* First, I would like to thank Bryce Walker and his staff at Cassette Duplicators, Inc., who taped the seminar I did in Salt Lake City in February 1992 on the topic of dealing with differences in marriage. The two-hour audiocassette program provided the basic outline for this book.

I would like to thank Richard Tice once again for his editing. He has an unusual gift for understanding the use of words. (What few differences Richard and I had over the editing process of *Dealing with Differences* were easily resolved.) Many others were involved in the book production process. I'm grateful to Carole Cole, Sheri Dew, Richard Erickson, Tonya Facemyer, Craig Geertsen, Ronald Millett, Camille Olson, Linda Nimori, Patricia Parkinson, Richard Peterson, and Anne Sheffield for all they have done in bringing this book to completion.

Particular thanks to Chanalin Smith, a teaching assistant at Brigham Young University, who provided valuable insights and suggestions in the preparation of the manuscript. Thanks also to Tammi Hosman and Rachelle Moon, also teaching assistants, for their help.

My thanks to Dr. Terrance D. Olson, a personal friend and the chairman of the Department of Family Sciences at Brigham Young University, for his support and encouragement. Thanks also to Bea Jasperson and JanaLee Romrell, members of the Family Sciences staff, for their encouragement as well.

Special thanks to my seven children, Doug, Tammy, Brian, Jon, Jason, Kris, and Brandon, all of whom have collectively and individually introduced me to the broader scope of learning to deal with differences as a family.

And finally, I'm particularly grateful to my wife, Susan, who has struggled with me for twenty-eight years, at times unknowingly, through the ten Cs of dealing with differences, long before we identified the strategies or knew what they were. (After reviewing the final manuscript, Susan informed me we could have a near perfect marriage if we would just do things her way.)

May all married couples learn from their frustrations and setbacks and appreciate the growth and experience that comes from learning to deal with differences as they occur in marriage. My hope and prayer are that this book will assist in the process.

PART 1

DIFFERENCES AND THEIR EFFECTS ON MARRIAGE

1

INTRODUCTION

It was a hot August afternoon. My family and I had driven up Provo Canyon to Aspen Grove Camp, which is owned and operated by Brigham Young University. During the three days at the camp, I was to give four speeches on marriage and family life for those attending.

My first speech given the evening we arrived went rather well. The next day I was scheduled to give one talk in the morning and one in the afternoon right after lunch. The next morning, after my early presentation, the husbands and wives headed out to hike, rapell, or do whatever they chose. They came back, had lunch, and gathered in the lodge at 1:30 P.M. for my third lecture.

As soon as I stood up, I realized we were in for a long sixty minutes. It was not only hot outside but warm in the lodge as well, and a few flies buzzed around the room. Those in attendance were full of food from the fine lunch prepared for them and tired from the morning activities.

Not long after I began, three or four people dozed off. A few others seemed more intent on swatting flies. Some listened politely, who I suspected had learned to sleep with their eyes open. But one woman sat at the back of the room and listened intently. At first I didn't notice her, but as the time ticked slowly away for all of us, I saw she was taking notes as fast as she could.

It became obvious halfway through my sixty-minute presentation that the audience was anxious to get back out into the mountains and trails for the afternoon activities. (I've since learned not to give after-dinner speeches, or to keep them won-derfully short.) In an effort to stir some life into the speech and group, I decided to try out some new thoughts and ideas. So I put my notes down and made a few observations about contem-porary marriage that brought a thunderous round of silence.

After a few more tries I finally made the following obser-vation: "A good marriage is not determined by how much we are originally alike. A good marriage is determined by how many differences we can learn to tolerate in each other." There were one or two nods of approval as the sleepers began to wake from their naps. By then my time was up, and the group left. A few made some polite remarks about "having enjoyed the talk."

Finally they all had gone but one — the woman at the back who had paid attention and even taken notes. As I prepared to leave, she asked, "Dr. Barlow, can I talk to you for a moment?" I agreed, and she said, "I really appreciated that thought about a good marriage."

I didn't know which one it was since I had tried out several new ones. Somewhat embarrassed, I asked, "Which thought was that?"

She replied, "The one about learning to tolerate differences in each other." She related how she and her husband, both active Latter-day Saints, were on the verge of divorce. They, like many other LDS couples, had started out with high hopes and expec-tations of themselves and their marriage. But as twenty years of marriage came and passed, a great many differences had emerged between them. Part of their differences were over his employ-ment, which demanded much of his time and energy. She said they differed on how to rear their children and how to live the gospel, and she listed several other differences that had developed *during* their marriage. Their differences now seemed so numerous and pronounced that they were planning divorce. They had decided to attend the Aspen Grove Camp as a last family outing with their children and then inform them when it was over that they were going to divorce.

"Do you really think," she asked with tears welling in her

eyes, "that my husband and I can learn to tolerate the differences that exist in our marriage?" We talked for a few more minutes as she listed some of their differences that were painful to experience. Finally I said, "Yes, I do believe you can."

"But how do you learn to deal with differences in marriage?" she asked. That was a good question, and I gave her the few general guidelines I had at the time. Later that evening she asked me to spend a few minutes with her and her husband. She had gone back to the cabin and shared with him the things we had discussed about dealing with the many differences she had identified. As we sat near the campfire that night, I shared one or two other insights I had about dealing with differences in marriage. By then I had realized that the topic needed more attention and investigation on my part.

When our three days at camp ended, they informed me that they had decided not to divorce immediately. The couple wanted to go home and try a few of the suggestions before making the decision. As they piled their camping gear and kids into their van and drove off, I began to comprehend the significance of what had happened, not only for the couple, but for their children as well.

I have never forgotten that afternoon presentation and the conversations that followed. For that husband and wife I had unintentionally made one small observation that was at the very center of their marital problems. I don't know what happened to the couple. Maybe they did divorce later on. But at least they had decided to delay the decision until they tried a few suggestions on dealing with their marital differences.

That one experience more than any other is responsible for this book. In my counseling experiences and classes since then, I have realized more clearly than ever before that learning to deal with differences in marriage is not just something to consider, but is actually an absolute necessity for surviving in contemporary marriage.

Learning to deal with differences is particularly critical for Latter-day Saints for at least three major reasons: (1) As noted in my book *Just for Newlyweds,* the divorce rate in the United States for young couples is expected to exceed 50 percent, and the disruption of marriages (divorce plus abandonment) may well reach a rate of two-thirds in the decade ahead.[1] (2) Some Latter-day Saints have come to believe that "oneness" means "sameness." (3) Others in the LDS community, including my wife, Susan, and myself, have grown up with the conflict-free marriage model.

The conflict-free marriage model suggests that happily married couples do not or should not have differences or disagreements. After several years of experiencing the idiosyncrasies of marriage, counseling others, and teaching about marriage, I can assure you that nearly all happily married couples do have differences! They have just learned how to work through the ones that are either present at the time of marriage or emerge as the years go by.

Church leader and humorist Elder J. Golden Kimball noted the difficulty of a couple living without some differences of opinion or conflict. He jokingly observed, "I have often wondered what would happen if a perfect man married a perfect woman. I'll bet he would shoot her inside of a week if she didn't poison him first."[2] The conflict-free marriage is a process to be learned rather than a state of being. That has been the case in our own marriage, as I will later note, and it is true for most other married couples as well.

A PERCH MARRIED TO A SPARROW?

Suppose that a perch were married to a sparrow. What kind of marriage would they have? Or what if a swan were married to a goldfish, a duck to a trout, a carp to a turkey, or an eagle to a salmon? Can't you just imagine what kind of discussions they would have about the food they ate, how they traveled, and how comfortable they were in the environment? Would they have difficulty communicating? What characteristics would one have that might irritate the other? The possibilities for differences between the combinations of fish and birds seem endless.

And yet, that is the very metaphor President Spencer W.

Kimball used when he admonished Latter-day Saint couples to try to resolve their differences. In his famous "Fish and Fowl" analogy, he noted:

> Most couples surmount problems. Perhaps you have thought that your home was the one home that was frustrated. You should know that most couples have their problems, that many couples master their problems, instead of permitting the problems to crush them. I think that most wives have shed bitter tears, and most husbands have lain sleepless hours over misunderstandings, but thanks be to the Lord that great numbers of these people have solved their difficulties. Partners stay in business together for years and years. *They may be as different as fish and fowl,* but because there is a great reason for their understanding of each other, they overlook each others' weaknesses, strengthen themselves, and work together. They seldom ever break up a partnership where they would both lose seriously by doing so. A celestial marriage is far more to fight for and to live for and adjust for, than any amount of money that two partners might have between them.[3]

Dealing with differences in marriage, therefore, warrants some thought and attention for all married couples, both young and old, especially when they are as different as birds and fish. To this end, and to the Latter-day Saint couple I met at Aspen Grove Camp on that August day, this book is written.

THE IMPORTANCE
OF DIFFERENCES

Not long after I received my Ph.D. in marriage and family relations from Florida State University, I attended a convention in Portland, Oregon, of the National Council on Family Relations. This event was of particular interest to me because Dr. David R. Mace and his wife, Vera, were scheduled to give a presentation in one of the sessions.

All during my training at Florida State University I had heard about David and Vera Mace. I had read with great interest about the Association of Couples for Marriage Enrichment, which they started in the 1960s. It was a new movement to help couples maintain and appreciate what was working well in their marriages and also to help prevent major problems from arising.

When the time came for the Maces' two-hour seminar, the room was crowded with professional marriage counselors, anxious to hear firsthand what the couple would say. The Maces were now in their seventies, and they had done much good throughout the world in promoting the stability and well-being of marriage.

Vera Mace spoke first, sharing a few insights about what she and her husband had learned about marriages in other countries. When David Mace stood up, he asked, "If you had just one hour to help any couple with their marriage, what would you do?" He then called on several to respond.

One young woman said she would help them with communication skills. Another man said he would help them understand the importance of physical and emotional intimacy. Others focused on equally important areas in marriage. I wondered what I would say if called upon.

Finally, Dr. Mace stated that after fifty years of experience in counseling he had come to believe there was one area more crucial than any other. If he had only one hour to assist a couple with their marriage, he would help them resolve the anger that arises between married couples. He and his wife spent the remainder of their time explaining why they thought anger was an important topic to consider.

David Mace made two statements during that session that startled many of us, including all the Latter-day Saints who were in the audience. He stated: (1) Marriage generates more "opportunity" for anger than any other relationship. (2) People become more angry with a husband or wife than with any other person.

He elaborated by explaining that we often become irritated, annoyed, or angry with people we care about the most. This is particularly true with spouses or children. We are around them much of the time and care about what happens to them. This is what he meant by "opportunity" for anger. This is particularly true in the husband-wife relationship because spouses interact most with each other and have many areas of common interest and concern. Unless married couples learn to recognize and deal with the anger in their marriage, the anger keeps them from being loving and caring. The Maces suggested that adults have a difficult time experiencing two strong emotions simultaneously. When we are angry, we can't be loving, so until the anger is resolved, we will not or cannot love in the way most of us would like to love.[1]

Before concluding their presentation, the Maces wrote four words on the chalkboard with arrows in between:

Differences ◊ Disagreements ◊ Conflict ◊ Anger

They noted that differences can lead to disagreements, which can lead to conflict, which can lead to anger. After documenting the danger of prolonged anger in a marriage, they suggested that couples should learn to deal with the differences that can and do arise in marriage. By so doing, they could avoid to some degree the end result of anger. It was the first and perhaps one of the best insights I have received on the importance of dealing with differences in marriage.

Since that session, I have thought much about the problem of anger in marriage. I have studied David Mace's writings on the subject, and when I wrote *Twelve Traps in Today's Marriage and How to Avoid Them,* I wrote one chapter called "The Temper Trap" that included some of his observations on the importance of learning to resolve anger in a marital relationship.[2] I have often thought that today one more word ought to be added to the four-word sequence:

Differences ▷ Disagreement ▷ Conflict ▷ Anger ▷ Divorce

Is it possible that many if not most divorces in this country are a result of unattended differences? I think so. (I share some thoughts about divorce in chapter three.) Divorce trends indicate that married couples must learn to deal with differences in a way that will prevent subsequent disagreements, conflict, anger, and ultimately divorce.

IF YE ARE NOT ONE

Learning to deal with differences and the possible consequences in marriage is particularly critical to Latter-day Saints. When speaking to LDS couples, I often ask this question: "Do you get angry at your spouse?" No one wants to admit that he or she does. So I ask another question: "Do you become irritated or 'ticked off' at your husband or wife?" Almost everyone laughs and acknowledges that once in a while they do. After a little more discussion, most will admit that, on occasion, they get very irritated.

Becoming angry doesn't mean that anger is or should be

appropriate. But as mortal beings we sometimes do get angry at neighbors, friends, children, and spouses. The interesting thing is, why are we so hesitant to admit it? Perhaps because in many Christian communities, anger is viewed as a lack of spiritual development. Many Church members may feel that admitting they become angry suggests spiritual inferiority.

There is a scriptural passage that haunts many LDS couples who become entangled in differences, disagreements, and conflict: "I say unto you, be one; and if ye are not one ye are not mine." (D&C 38:27.) Some Latter-day Saints have interpreted this to mean that we must all be the same: that "oneness equals sameness." If this is true, then any differences, disagreements, or conflicts that arise in a marriage would suggest that the couple are not yet "one" and therefore are not yet the Lord's.

On this misunderstanding, Orson Pratt noted, "What are we to understand by two becoming one flesh? [Genesis 2:24.] Does it mean that the male and female lose their identity as persons? By no means. Such a circumstance never happened in any age of the world. Does it mean that they become one merely in thoughts, affections, and minds? No; it says they twain shall be one flesh; mark the expression, *'one flesh,'* not one mind."[3]

Anger does affect our ability to do or dwell on spiritual things. (See Matthew 5:21–26.) Even in the temple we are asked in a certain place not to participate if we have ill feelings toward anyone. I believe that becoming one is a process that takes time and effort because differences, disagreements, conflict, and anger surface in every LDS marriage. But this does not mean the Lord has given up on us.

An experience from the lives of the Prophet Joseph Smith and his wife, Emma, is indicative of how anger affects us and how it may be dealt with. David Whitmer, an associate of Joseph and Emma, noted an incident that occurred in the Whitmer home in 1829 when Joseph was translating the Book of Mormon:

> One morning when he [Joseph] was getting ready to continue the translation, something went wrong about the

house and he was put out about it. Something that Emma, his wife, had done. Oliver and I went upstairs and Joseph came up soon after to continue the translation but he could not do anything. He could not translate a single syllable. He went downstairs, out into the orchard, and made supplication to the Lord; was gone about an hour — came back to the house, and asked Emma's forgiveness and then came upstairs where we were and then the translation went on all right.[4]

If the Prophet Joseph and Emma had to learn to deal with their differences, so must we.

IMPORTANCE FOR NEWLYWEDS

Learning to deal with differences in marriage is important for all married couples, no matter how long they have been married. But newlyweds in particular, like Joseph and Emma, who had been married only two years, need to learn to work out their differences soon after they are married. This is not something a couple would discuss on the honeymoon or during the first few months of marriage (I discuss why on on page 71). However, for some very good reasons, it is something the couple should work at diligently within the first year or two.

One of those reasons is the alarming trend of early divorces in the United States and in Utah. Note these statistics:

1. Approximately 7 percent of divorces in Utah occur before one year of marriage.

2. The highest divorce rates in Utah are in the first and second year, when 11 percent of the divorces occur each year.

3. Thirty-eight percent of Utah's divorces are granted to couples married three years or less. This follows a trend in the United States for the divorce rate to peak after three years of marriage.

4. Over half (nearly 54 percent) of Utah's divorces occur within the first five years of marriage.[5]

Since so many divorces are occurring in Utah and in the rest of the nation fairly soon after marriage, then the sequence leading to it (differences ◊ disagreements ◊ conflict ◊ anger ◊ divorce) must also be occurring fairly early for many couples. Soon after they marry, therefore, newlyweds should learn the skills to deal effectively with differences if many of the divorces are to be avoided.

THE 80/20 PHENOMENA

One of the texts I use in my marriage preparation course at BYU contains an interesting observation that the students appreciate very much:

> Many people expect that their partner will meet all of their needs, indeed that it is the partner's duty to do this. To the extent that partners fail to live up to this expectation, they are "bad" spouses. But human beings are complex, and it is probably impossible for any two people to meet one another's needs completely. If a couple could mutually satisfy even 80 percent of each other's needs, it would be a minor miracle.
>
> The expectation of total need fulfillment within marriage ruins many marital relationships. As time passes, the spouse with the unmet needs will long to have them satisfied and will accuse the partner of failure and indifference. Conflict will grow because the accused spouse feels unfairly accused, defensive, and inferior. Life will revolve more and more around the unfulfilled 20 percent. This is especially true if the partners are possessive and block each other from any outside need gratification. Unless such a pattern of interaction is broken, a spouse may suddenly fall out of love and leave the mate for someone else. These sudden departures are catastrophic to all the parties. And the ensuing relationship often fails because of the same dynamics. For example, the dissatisfied spouse finds a person who meets some of the unfulfilled needs and, because these needs have become so exaggerated, concludes that at last he or she has met the "right" person. In all the excitement, the person often overlooks the fact that the new love does not fulfill other needs that have long been met by the discarded spouse. In a few years the conflicts will reappear over different unmet needs, and the process of disenchantment will recur.[6]

I have had students tell me that this one thought alone is worth the price of a rather expensive college textbook. We discuss in class that we are expected, as Latter-day Saints, to meet our sexual needs and our most critical needs for companionship only with our spouses. We have no license to seek them elsewhere. But we need to realize that, as Cox suggests, if our husbands or wives meet 80 percent of our needs, we should be grateful! Rather than focus on the 80 percent of our needs that are met, we often become preoccupied with the 20 percent that are unmet. And that makes us miserable.

This thought is particularly significant to single men and women who are choosing a marriage partner. They may be seeking companions who will meet *all* their needs. And for a while, romance and passion trick them into thinking they have found that person. But as they soon find out, during courtship or early in the marriage, their companions are very good people who are able to meet 80 or even 90 percent of their needs, but not all. Some single people never marry because of the mistaken view that leads them to search for a person who will meet 100 percent of their needs. After reading this thought, many of my students realize that they are dating good people who will make good husbands or wives but that some part of their prospective marriage partners, 20 percent more or less, will remain mysterious, hard to understand, or perhaps even a bit strange at times.

Dr. James Dobson, in his book *Love for a Lifetime,* has observed: "Two people are not compatible simply because they love each other and both are professing Christians. Many young couples assume that the sunshine and flowers that characterized their courtship will continue for the rest of their lives. . . . It is naïve to expect two unique and strong-willed individuals to mesh together like a couple of machines. Even gears have multiple cogs with rough edges to be honed before they will work in concert."[7] He then asks this question of wives:

> Can you accept the fact that your husband will never be
> able to meet all your needs and aspirations? Seldom does

one human being satisfy every longing and hope in the breast of another. Obviously, this coin has two sides: You can't be his perfect woman, either. He is no more equipped to resolve your entire package of emotional needs than you are to become his sexual dream machine every twenty-four hours. Both partners have to settle for human foibles and faults and irritability and fatigue and occasional nighttime "headaches." A good marriage is not one where perfection reigns: It is a relationship where a healthy perspective over-looks a multitude of "unresolvables."[8]

Perhaps the mix of needs met in your marriage will be 80/20, 90/10, or 70/30. Some claim you can even survive in marriage if 60 percent of your needs are met. But whatever the proportion, we must learn to focus on what we have and receive rather than on what we don't have and what we want. The Bible states "Whatsoever things are true, whatsoever things are honest, what-soever things are just, whatsoever things are pure, whatsoever things are lovely, whatsoever things are of good report; if there be any virtue, and if there be any praise, *think on these things.*" (Philippians 4:8; italics added.)

UNATTENDED DIFFERENCES: THE PATHWAY TO DIVORCE

Most people today are aware of the chaotic condition of marriage in the United States and in other countries as well. Since the majority (52 percent) of marriages in the U.S. are ending in divorce, divorce has become the norm. This also suggests that staying with someone in the first marriage is becoming the exception. For those marrying since 1970, the divorce rates are projected to be even higher — with a 56 percent rate for legal divorce and a 6 percent rate of abandonment or nonlegal separation. This would be a 62 percent, or nearly two-thirds, combined disruption rate of contemporary marriages.[1]

DIVORCE IS AN EPIDEMIC

I have spoken to dozens of Latter-day Saint audiences about marriage and often remarked that if I were allowed only two minutes to give an insight on contemporary marriage, I would read one verse of scripture: "Others will he [Satan] pacify, and lull them away into carnal security, that they will say: All is well in Zion; yea, Zion prospereth, all is well — and thus the devil cheateth their souls, and leadeth them away carefully down to hell." (2 Nephi 28:21.)

President Spencer W. Kimball was president of the Quorum of the Twelve and later President of the Church during the 1970s and early '80s when the divorce rate rapidly escalated in the United States. During this time he noted that many divorces could be avoided if the couples seriously worked at improving the relationship. He stated: "I know there are many who feel that they have been justified [in divorce], and there may have been some who were justified. We are not talking to them or of them. We are talking of the great majority that could have been salvaged, could have been saved if we had tried and tried hard enough."[2] As President of the Church, he later noted: "We are concerned over the mounting number of divorces not only in our society, but in the Church. We are just as concerned with those whose families and marriages seem to be held together in 'quiet desperation.' "[3]

The Church leader stated that not only is divorce itself a problem, but the widespread acceptance of it is of even greater concern: "Divorce is not a cure for difficulty, but is merely an escape, and a weak one. . . . The divorce itself does not constitute the entire evil, but the very acceptance of divorce as a cure is also a serious sin of this generation. Because a program or a pattern is universally accepted is not evidence that it is right. *Marriage never was easy. It may never be*. It brings with it sacrifice, sharing and a demand for great selflessness."[4]

President Ezra Taft Benson has similarly noted: "The family has serious problems. *Divorce is epidemic*. The incidence of delinquency is on the rise. The answer is not more marriage counselors or social workers. The answer lies in a husband and wife taking their marriage covenant seriously, realizing that they both have a responsibility to make their marriage a happy one."[5]

IS DIVORCE EVER JUSTIFIED?

Many Church members wonder if divorce is ever justified. The answer is simply "yes." Extremely unwise choices or mistakes will sometimes be made in choosing marriage partners, particularly if such choices are made in haste or made when the partners are very young. Severe changes may also occur in personality or behaviors that make the continuation of the marriage especially difficult. Some couples may be "unequally yoked" at the time of the marriage. Others can become so with time. (See 2 Corinthians 6:14.)

Even when teaching against the rampant divorce of their time, Jesus and the Apostle Paul mentioned some exceptions. (See Matthew 19:9; 1 Corinthians 7:10–15.) Rodney Turner, professor emeritus of religion at Brigham Young University, made this observation on divorce:

> Pretense — maintaining appearances for appearances sake — meant nothing to Jesus. He was a realist. Although he taught that divorce was contrary to the will of heaven, He nevertheless allowed for it under certain circumstances. God permits divorce in fact; he does not condone it *in principle*. Forbidding divorce on any grounds whatsoever is both unscriptural and immoral. The Lord would not have given the Church the authority to bind and to *loose* if such were the case [Matthew 16:19; 18:18; D&C 132:45, 46]. . . . Human judgment is fallible — especially when we are young and inexperienced. Mistakes are made. Nothing is gained by perpetuating a relationship which is hopelessly wrong. . . . An enduring relationship — whether with God or man — cannot be coerced; it must be achieved without compulsory means — being founded upon the natural harmony of its component parts.[6]

In the April 1991 general conference, President Gordon B. Hinckley discussed the plague of divorce, saying: "There may be now and again a legitimate cause for divorce. I am not one to say that it is never justified. But I say without hesitation that this plague among us, which seems to be growing everywhere, is not of God, but rather the work of the adversary of righteousness and peace and truth."[7] In the same conference address he also noted, "Some of you within the sound of my voice could recount family sorrows in your own experience. But among the greatest tragedies, and I think the most common, is divorce. It has become as a great scourge."[8]

WHY SO MANY DIVORCES?

Why are there so many divorces today? One response that might come to the minds of many Latter-day Saints is that the trend is a sign of the last days. Jesus noted that prior to the Second Coming, relationships, along with many other aspects of life, would deteriorate ánd fail. Many would deceive one another, hate one another, betray one another, and the love of many would wax cold. (See Matthew 24:3–4, 10, 12; see also 2 Timothy 3:1–4 for similar signs of the times in the last days.)

As did President Hinckley, others would attribute many of the chaotic conditions of contemporary marriages to the work of Satan, who is the father of contention (see 3 Nephi 11:29) and who seeks to make others miserable as he himself is miserable (see 2 Nephi 2:27). Some would even suggest that Satan works extra hard on Latter-day Saint marriages because he is at war with the Saints and has us encompassed about. (See D&C 76:29.) If possible, he wants to deceive the very elect. (See Matthew 24:24.) So subtle is Satan that in the last days he will try to convince us that he and his influence do not exist, lulling us into complacency until he can grasp us "with his awful chains." (2 Nephi 28:22.) Many of us he leads about carefully with the flaxen cord, or light thread, until he has us bound. (See 2 Nephi 26:22.) He will try to pacify us and trick us into thinking "all is well" in our marriages when we really may be on the pathway to marital destruction. (2 Nephi 28:21.)

However cunning and crafty Satan may be in the last days, not all the marital disruption and discord can or should be attributed to him and his followers. Many of the marital mishaps today can be attributed to our own ineptness or lack of effort, skills, or commitment. Many marriages too have become marriages of "convenience"—that is, the couples have agreed, openly or within their hearts, to live together in business-like relationships, or even in the "quiet desperation" previously noted by President Kimball. Along these lines, President Kimball also observed that "many couples permit their marriages to become stale and their love to grow cold like old bread or worn-out jokes or cold gravy."[9]

Divorced spouses are not always equally responsible for the deterioration of the marriage. One marriage partner might be a caring, committed, faithful spouse while the other is not. In the case of sin, a husband or wife may have committed grievous errors, such as adultery, while the marriage partner was faithful. The divorced spouses may not be in equal need of repentance, and one may be relatively blameless. Care should be taken not to make hasty judgments and insinuations.

THE PATHWAY TO DIVORCE

Are there some steps along the way toward marital disruption that a couple can learn to recognize? How can a couple tell if their marriage is on the pathway to divorce? This is a particularly significant question for Latter-day Saints who have made sacred covenants in holy temples to be together for eternity. But first they must survive mortality as a married couple.

It is obvious to many marriage counselors and educators today that married couples don't just "get divorced." Divorce is more of a process that involves three phases: (1) an emotional detachment or separation, followed by (2) a physical separation or a sequence of separations, ending with (3) the event of legal divorce, or termination of the relationship. Divorce is seldom a quick, spontaneous, spur-of-the-moment decision. In most cases it is the culmination of a long period of gradual alienation covering many months, or sometimes years, that began with the first serious thought of divorce and built to the final legal decree.

In a chapter titled "Falling in and out of Love" from her book *Solutions,* Leslie Cameron-Bandler identifies three stages of "falling in love," the importance of maintaining a loving relationship, and five stages of "falling out of love."[10] Understanding these stages may help couples reinforce the "falling in love" process and avoid or break away from the "falling out of love" sequence.

How Love Begins

The author of *Solutions* notes three stages of how love begins: (1) attraction, (2) appreciation, and (3) habituation.

1. *Attraction:* Among the many people we meet, there are

some to whom we are more attracted than others. Something about a person's physical appearance, clothing, hair fashion or style, personality, certain mannerisms, or other traits strikes us as more desirable than another person's appearance or personality. The person might have a skill or talent, a way of smiling, some form of touching, a gift, a likable familiarity, an ability to listen or do some things that make them particularly attractive.

2. *Appreciation:* If the attraction is maintained long enough, and if certain desirable acts are repeated frequently, the acts are generally acknowledged and in some way returned. The acknowledgment may be a simple comment of appreciation such as "Thank you" or "I appreciate what you did," or a hug, or a kiss, or a return favor.

3. *Habituation:* When the acts of love or kindness are repeated often, a couple finds their expectations or needs more fully met. They begin to pursue and eventually commit to an ongoing relationship, which may culminate in marriage. The key to this stage is to repeat the desired behaviors often enough so that the other person continues to be attracted and to feel appreciated. Showing deeds of love infrequently will not suffice; they must be repeated often. (See 1 Corinthians 13:4–7; Moroni 7:45–48 for scriptural definitions of love.)

How Love Ends

Leslie Cameron-Bandler notes the following five stages of how love ends:

1. *Expectation:* While a couple is "in love" in their marriage, they focus on the satisfactions they experience. However, a subtle shift can occur, according to Cameron-Bandler, when one or both spouses start focusing on what is not there and on what he or she thinks should be there but isn't. The number of complaints increases while the number of compliments decreases. The couple come to expect much, or more, and appreciate little. They spend more and more time dwelling on their perceptions or *beliefs* that their expectations are not being met. They begin to feel unloved,

uncared for, or unwanted. This may occur to either or both spouses.

2. *Disappointment/disillusionment:* Once a couple begin to focus on specific needs not being met in the marriage, they tend to generalize in other areas of the relationship. They perceive disappointments or disillusionments where they had been satisfied before. The disappointments may actually have existed previously, but they had not seemed important or worth noticing. The spouse remembers more pleasant and "better times" in the marriage and begins to perceive his or her partner as being less lovable, more uncaring, or more disrespectful. During this stage the deeds of kindness and love may actually become less frequent or less spontaneous. In addition, a spouse's negative traits become more pronounced or noticeable.

Still, in this stage, there is the desire to recapture the joys and fulfillments of the past. Despite the disappointments and disillusionment, the couple, alone or with the help of a caring church leader, or a skilled marriage counselor or therapist, will frequently restore their love and commitment.

3. *Threshold:* At some point in the relationship either the husband or wife will reach a point where he or she believes the relationship is over. The spouse believes that the relationship is no longer worthwhile because the marriage partner cannot or will not provide the desired fulfillment. By now the person has reached "threshold." Memories of past fulfillments fade and are soon forgotten.

4. *Perceptual reorientation:* After threshold, the spouse goes through a perception change or reorientation, identifying more with the present disappointments and pains than with any "good times," present or past. Common statements during this stage are "It's too late; there isn't anything we can do," or "Now I know him for what he really is" or "If she did nice things in the past, she really didn't mean them." The interesting fact is that "things" do not often change radically during this time, but how they are perceived changes markedly. The spouse going through perceptual reorientation usually gives up. Even more tragic is the

fact that the other spouse may not have given up yet. One spouse wants to work at improving the relationship while the one who is at threshold or perceptual reorientation sees little need in making any effort.

5. *Verification:* A spouse who reaches the stage of verification begins looking for behaviors, words, or habits that will vindicate his or her perceptions. Not only will the spouse try to verify them individually, he or she will often try to "prove" them to the marriage partner. A spouse might also solicit the verification of family and friends to substantiate those perceptions. Couples at this stage sometimes make long lists, mentally or written, of the perceived unwanted behavior of each other. Such lists act as proof that the supposedly offending spouse is actually "that way." At this point a lawyer or attorney may be contacted to give legal verification of the spouse's perceptions, and the final phase of terminating the marriage begins.

WORKING AT MARRIAGE

Though any married couple, young or old, may experience marital problems and concerns, even to the point of contemplating divorce, couples should not give up too soon. Both LDS and secular authorities on marriage have urged contemporary couples to work earnestly at improving their relationship. A psychologist, Dr. Diane Medved, in her excellent book, *The Case against Divorce,* has admonished, "If you hear someone for whom you have any feeling at all hinting at separation, instead of tacitly endorsing the move, instantly protest. Nearly every marriage has something worth preserving, something that can be restored. Revitalizing a relationship brings triumph and ongoing reward; and as you'll see, avoiding divorce spares those concerned from the greatest trauma of their lives."[11]

Similarly, President Kimball also noted, "While marriage is difficult, and discordant and frustrated marriages are common, yet real, lasting happiness is possible, and marriage can be more an exultant ecstasy than the human mind can conceive. This is within the reach of every couple, every person."[12]

Elder Dean L. Larsen has also given this insight into working on a marital relationship: "I am convinced that there is something so absolutely sacred in the eyes of the Lord about the marriage covenant that he expects us to devote every energy and resource in our power to make our marriages endure. For those who do, even in the face of great challenges and difficulties, I am certain there will be ultimate blessings realized that are beyond our present comprehension."[13]

LDS has become known as the acronym for Latter-day Saints. Perhaps it could also stand for "Let's do something!" Let's do something about our marriages and the differences that emerge! Let's work earnestly to build harmonious relationships with those we love. And may we all be more careful to not allow ourselves to be led . . . or to lead ourselves . . . down the pathway of marital discord or even destruction.

SOURCES OF DIFFERENCES

Where do the differences that emerge in every marriage come from? What is their source? I've been able to identify at least five categories of sources: individual differences, family-of-origin differences, male/female differences, community differences, and religious differences. Let's consider each one separately.

INDIVIDUAL DIFFERENCES

Any individual knows that he or she is quite different from anyone else. Differences existed even among Jesus' disciples. Because of individual personality traits and characteristics, the disciples didn't always agree among themselves. In Luke 17:1–10 the Savior gave a lesson on forgiveness and overcoming offenses. He told his disciples that "it is impossible but that offences will come." (Verse 1.) He encouraged them to forgive each other as many as seven times in one day. On another occasion the mother of James and John came to a meeting of the apostles and asked Jesus to grant that her two sons might sit on his right and on his left in the kingdom. She wanted her two sons to preside over the others. What was the response? "And when the ten heard it, they were moved with indignation against the two brethren." (Matthew 20:24; see 20–28 for the entire account.)

By living in a family, a neighborhood, a ward, a community, and a nation, we inevitably give and receive offenses. It is "impossible" for us not to experience this. Thus we should not be surprised that husbands and wives will differ on occasion in preferences and plans. One common saying notes that "if two people always agree, one is unnecessary." The challenge, then, is for married couples to learn to deal with the differences that arise. Some young people encounter their differences early in marriage and start thinking things like "If I had only married so and so, these things would not have happened." They do not realize that there will always be differences regardless of whom one marries.

One of the interesting questions in the study of child development is, How much do parents and the social environment influence a child? Some believe in "parental determinism," which suggests that parents largely determine what children become. Metaphorically, children are supposedly born with clean slates on which their fathers and mothers write, giving children the direction they take. There seems to be some evidence for this theory.

Others suggest that certain personality traits or characteristics are present at birth. Since Latter-day Saints believe in a premortal life (see Abraham 3:22–26; Jeremiah 1:5), they also believe that every man and woman attained a different level of obedience and knowledge there. Is it not possible that some of our traits and characteristics come with us to this life?

An LDS psychologist who works a great deal with LDS youth and teenagers told me one time that he couldn't figure out why certain rebellious children came from "good" LDS homes and parents. He finally concluded that a part of every person's character was formed in the premortal state and that every person brought that character into mortality. Some parents, he decided, must simply inherit difficult children. We may never know in this life whether or not his observations are true, but they do provide an interesting explanation of certain conditions we experience in mortality.

The fact that all the children in a single family manifest different tastes, personality traits, and behavior when they are infants indicates that not all these things are learned. Yet, the experiences and nurturing that children receive shape them from the moment of first interaction with another person. By the time they are adults, they have built complex histories, acquired unique sets of experiences, and developed makeups that distinguish them sharply from each other. One of the most common misassumptions couples make when courting is to assume that the handful of interests and values they share make them alike in all ways.

FAMILY-OF-ORIGIN DIFFERENCES

Couples learn soon after they marry that each spouse brings a different perspective to the relationship from his or her family of origin. This was true in our marriage. Susan was raised as an only child. I had one older sister, Jane, and one younger, Karen. Will a girl who is brought up alone have a differing view of marriage and family from an only boy who grows up with two sisters?

Then there is the question of sibling order. Are there certain characteristics of the oldest child? An only child? The youngest? The middle child? A younger brother of sisters? An older sister of brothers? The answer to all these questions is, Yes, sibling order does make a difference that may require some assessment and adjustment after marriage.[1]

In addition, much of what we know about marriage we observe from our own parents as we grow up. They are our primary marriage model until we learn from other sources, such as peers, the media, education, and religious instruction, other ways to be married. It is only natural, therefore, that a couple will face differing and sometimes conflicting ideas or traditions soon after they are married.

For instance, Susan and I had two different parental marriage models. Susan's mother, Alice, had a deal worked out with her husband, Cecil, that she would do the cooking and he would wash the dishes. The arrangement of dishwashing worked fine for them. My mother, Ruth, was a busy schoolteacher and liked to work in her own kitchen. My father, Alvin, was gone a lot because of truck driving and church work. So he rarely helped wash the dishes. When they had a party or guests, my dad would always help in the kitchen, but most of the time, Mom was the one who did the dishes. There are few women on this earth who could wash dishes faster than my mother. As soon as she finished eating, she started. If she was ready to wash your plate, you had better be finished eating because it was gone. (Though my two sisters usually helped in the kitchen, I frequently got a "headache" when it was my turn to do dishes.)

Do you get the picture? I grew up believing that wives, mothers, and sisters washed the dishes. What was Susan's perception? Women cook, and men wash dishes! You can imagine what our first year of marriage was like after meals. Neither of us then, or now, liked to do dishes. Finally we got a dishwasher, and then the issue became who would load it with dirty dishes.

Our first Christmas together we discovered one other pronounced difference. When we celebrated Christmas in my home, we opened the gifts from each other on Christmas Eve and opened the ones from Santa on Christmas morning. That seemed to me the sane way to celebrate Christmas. But in Susan's family, no one opened any gifts from anyone until Christmas morning! Only holiday heretics would think of doing otherwise. After we had children, Christmas became a fiasco in our home. Would we celebrate it Dad's way, or Mom's way? We finally agreed to do it her way one Christmas and my way the next. (See chapter ten on compromise.) It has reduced the tension somewhat, but I still think my way is the best way to celebrate Christmas. The only problem is, Susan feels just as strongly about her preference.

MALE/FEMALE DIFFERENCES

Most married couples soon discover that differences arise in marriage simply because one is male and one is female. During the past two decades some of the major differences between males and females have been researched and documented. As early as 1971, Dr. Paul Popenoe, founder of the American Institute for Family Relations in Los Angeles, detailed some of the differences between men and women. He noted the following:

1. Men and women differ in every cell of their bodies due to the chromosome combinations creating males and females.

2. Women usually outlive men by three or four years.

3. Women have a lower basal metabolism than do men.

4. Women differ in skeletal structure. For instance, a woman's first finger is usually longer than her third. Also, girls' teeth do not last as long as boys' teeth.

5. Women generally have larger stomachs, kidneys, livers, and appendixes but smaller lungs than men.

6. Women have more emotional swings because of menstruation, pregnancy, lactation, and menopause.

7. Women generally have larger thyroid glands than men, which makes them more resistant to colds and more prone to goiter. Because of this, they also have smoother skin and a relatively hairless body. The gland also produces a thin layer of subcutaneous fat, which contributes to important elements in personal beauty. A larger thyroid also makes many women less emotionally stable, causing them to laugh and cry more easily than men.

8. Women have blood with more water and fewer (20 percent) red blood cells supplying oxygen to body cells. Consequently, they often tire more easily and are more prone to faint.

9. Women generally have hearts that beat more rapidly and have lower blood pressure, at least until after menopause.

10. Women generally can stand, prefer, or are more comfortable in higher temperatures than are men. (That one insight may save much frustration in many marriages!)[2]

Ten years later, in her book *What Every Woman Should Know about Men*, Dr. Joyce Brothers asked and answered this interesting question: "Are men and women really so different? They are. They really are. I spent months talking to biologists, neurologists, geneticists, research psychiatrists, and psychologists. . . . What I discovered was that men are even more different from women than I had known. Their bodies are different and their minds are different. Men are different from the very composition of their blood to the way their brains develop, which means that they think and experience life differently from women."[3]

What, then, according to Dr. Brothers, are some of the major differences between men and women (some you may find rather surprising)? Men change their minds more often than women do. Men snore more. They have longer vocal cords. Men fight more and feel pain less than women do. Men lose weight more easily than women. Men are more often left-handed. They talk less about themselves but worry more about themselves. They are also less sensitive to others than women are.[4] Though sometimes we cannot tell if some of the differences are cultural or genetic, we have definitely learned that, though men and women are created equal, they are not the same.

In addition to these differences, Dr. Brothers reports that men and women do not think the same way. Their brains are very different. Each human brain is divided into two spheres or parts: the left brain and the right brain. The right brain (or hemisphere) governs the left side of the body and the left brain governs the right side of the body. Each side of the brain also controls different thought processes. The left hemisphere is the verbal brain, controlling language and reading skills. It processes information logically, step by step. We use the left brain to read, balance a checkbook, write letters, or figure our income taxes. The right brain or hemisphere works with space and how things are related to each other. We use this skill to move through a maze, assemble a jigsaw puzzle, design a house, or paint a picture.[5]

According to Dr. Brothers:

> Women are left-hemisphere [brain] oriented, more verbally adroit. The left hemisphere develops earlier, which gives them an edge in reading and writing. . . .
>
> Men use the right hemisphere more efficiently than women do. The converse is not true, however. Women do not use the left brain more efficiently than men. The male and female brains are by no means set up as mirror images of each other. What it adds up to is that we are blessed with two different ways of thinking and learning.

The male brain is specialized. Men use the right hemisphere when dealing with spatial problems and the left for
verbal problems. . . . The female brain is not specialized.
Right and left hemisphere work together on a problem. This
is possible because in the female brain left-hemisphere abilities are duplicated to some extent in the right hemisphere
and right-hemisphere abilities in the left. . . . The ability
to zero in on a problem with both hemispheres makes women
much more perceptive about people. [This is sometimes
called intuition.] They are better at sensing the difference
between what people say and what they mean and at picking
up the nuances that reveal another person's true feelings.[6]

Recent Research

Even more recently, some additional research on this topic
has been reported. In *Male and Female Realities: Understanding
the Opposite Sex*, Joe Tanenbaum has identified a number of broad,
general biological differences between males and females:

Sight. Women see better at night, whereas men see better
during the day. Women have fewer color perception problems.

Skin. The skin of women bruises more easily, possibly because
men have thicker skin. Men have coarser hair. The sweat glands
are distributed more evenly in women than in men. Women
wrinkle earlier.

Brain. Women have 40 percent more connectors in the brain
than men, and women have a larger corpus callosum and a larger
lower brain (the part most connected to emotions).

Body. Women are 23 percent muscle and 25 percent fat;
men, 40 percent muscle and 15 percent fat. The fat layer of
women is distributed more evenly than that of men, and women
burn fewer calories. They are more buoyant in water. Men have
stronger arms than women by 50 percent. Men have larger lungs.
In contrast, they have fewer nerve endings and a weaker immune
system than women.

Skeletal structure. Men have tighter, less flexible joints than
women. The bones of women are lighter, and they have smaller
hands and weaker thumbs. Men are 10 percent taller, and they

have thicker skulls that are larger at the base and smaller at the crown than those of women.

Development. More male babies than female babies are aborted, are born dead or blind, or die in the first three months. Female infants sit, walk, and talk sooner (girls experience advanced cell growth in the verbal hemisphere at age four). They are also less fretful, smile more, eat less, and control their bladders earlier. Spatial talents develop in males at age six; in females, at age thirteen. Diagnosed hyperactives are 90 percent male; dyslexics are 75 percent male. Men have a greater incidence of learning disorders, though women are more susceptible to alcohol abuse. At age sixty, women have 90 percent of the strength and flexibility they had at age twenty; men, 60 percent.[7]

Other research has focused on the male and female brain and the differences that arise from that. Anne Moir and David Jessel note, "The sexes are different because their brains are different. The brain, the chief administrative and emotional organ of life, is differently constructed in men and in women; it processes information in a different way, which results in different perceptions, priorities and behaviour. . . . It is time to explode the social myth that men and women are virtually interchangeable, all things being equal. All things are not equal."[8]

The basic facts couples should realize are that the differences between the sexes are real and that they must be taken into consideration in marriage. For instance, one article in *Time* magazine claims that "scientists are discovering that gender differences have as much to do with the biology of the brain as with the way we are raised." The author notes that more women focus their language skills in the front lobe while men focus language skills in the parietal, or upper posterior, part of the brain. Women have a thick bundle of nerves connecting the right and left hemispheres, which may allow for greater cross interactions between the two parts of the brain. This could be the basis for woman's intuition, which research, according to the article, indicates that many women do have. The hypothalamus in men is larger than that of women. This part of the brain is associated with sexual behavior.[9]

The same article suggests that men judge dimensions more accurately while women have better recall or memory capabilities. In one test, 64 percent of the males correctly matched three-dimensional objects compared to 41 percent of the females. Yet after looking at several objects in one group and then looking at another group, females were able to eliminate an average of fifteen objects not in the first group, and males, twelve. When given four words, over a three-minute span women came up with an average of 4.1 synonyms per word, while men came up with 2.2.[10]

In *You Just Don't Understand: Women and Men in Conversation*, Deborah Tannen writes that women and men have also been trained to use language differently. Girls grow up forming relations with other girls by giving and receiving information. They form groups by sharing and withholding secrets. On the other hand, boys form relationships and groups largely through activities. When girls become young women, they transfer the communication needs and skills to the young men they eventually marry. Dr. Tannen notes that there are "innumerable situations in which groundless allegations of . . . failings are made, simply because partners are expressing their thoughts and feelings, and their assumptions about how to communicate, in different ways. If we can sort out differences based on conversational style, we will be in a better position to confront real conflicts of interest — and to find a shared language in which to negotiate them."[11]

In *The Transparent Self*, psychologist Sidney Jourard also notes that women talk more than men and give and receive more information. With such talking women are able to convey some of their concerns and frustrations to others and thereby alleviate much of their stress. Men tend to keep their secrets and concerns bottled up inside. This, Jourard suggests, may be a major reason why women outlive men several years.[12]

COMMUNITY DIFFERENCES

Where a person is reared makes a difference how he or she behaves and thinks as an adult. Subsequently, it can and often does have an impact on the person's marriage. Besides growing up in a family, each individual associates with a larger community and incorporates some of the thoughts and characteristics of that community into his or her own personality.

I grew up in Centerfield, Utah, a town of six hundred people, and Susan grew up in San Luis Obispo, California. This has affected the kinds of places we've wanted to live in, the kinds of house we've wanted, and our adjustment to each of the places we have moved to. What if someone from Boston, Massachusetts, marries a person from rural Idaho? Both want to return to their native state to live. Should it make a difference? Would it make a difference?

Does it matter if a Northerner marries a Southerner? When I taught at Florida State University while working on my doctorate, one of my students from Georgia was surprised at her grandmother's response when she announced her engagement to a young man from New York. Her grandmother was concerned only with the fact that she was marrying a Yankee. Such a marriage could not prosper, the grandmother felt.

In the five universities where I have taught, I have noticed that international marriages have become fairly common. With so many students now attending colleges and universities outside their native countries, it is not surprising that the number of such marriages has naturally increased. Does it make a difference if someone from the U.S. marries someone from France or Germany? Are there beliefs and practices from the various countries that could or would make a difference in the marriage (besides the plane fares of flying home to spend a few days with the parents)?

Two years ago Susan and I had a chance to spend two days at the BYU–Hawaii campus at Laie on the island of Oahu, Hawaii. One afternoon while strolling around campus, we met a beautiful young woman from Samoa. When she found out I was a marriage counselor, she said she was in love with a returned missionary from Tonga. Her parents objected to the proposed marriage and wanted her to marry someone from Samoa. She asked me what I thought. I told her that all married couples have differences in their marriage regardless of the source. I asked her if there were any community practices in Tonga and Samoa that might later cause her and her fiancé some problems. She conceded that there were, in addition to some differences that could emerge from their two families of origin.

Of course, cultural and national differences do not necessarily mean that a couple should not get married. However, a couple need to take such differences into account and be prepared to deal with them should they marry.

RELIGIOUS DIFFERENCES

For my doctoral dissertation at Florida State University, I studied and wrote about interfaith marriages among the Latter-day Saints.[13] I had to make an extensive review of the literature regarding people who married members of different religious faiths. I found that many of the problems in such marriages arise not only from the theological beliefs, but also from the day-to-day living that comes with different religious groups.

For instance, how much, if any, money should be given to each church? How will we observe certain religious holidays? What foods will we eat or not eat? How often will we have religious functions in our home? Will we pray together or have family devotions? How much time will we spend in church activities? Will we participate as youth leaders, teachers, or administrators? What will we teach our children about our differing religious views?

While interfaith marriages are usually defined as marriages between two people from different faiths, differences could also arise over religious beliefs even if both husband and wife belonged to the same denomination. Many differences have to do with religiosity, or the degree to which one adheres to one's religious beliefs. One spouse could simply be more diligent than the other in living religious principles, and then all the questions mentioned in the previous paragraph would apply to such a couple.

Religion is far more than a set of abstract ideas about this life or the next. Religious beliefs involve daily behaviors that can cause many differences for a couple to deal with. This is particularly so when two people marry who belong to different religions and who are both deeply rooted in their faiths. As long as there are differing levels of commitment or adherence to religious beliefs, couples face possible disagreement and conflict.

BECOMING LESS TOLERANT WITH AGE?

As we grow older, we may become less tolerant, not only of ourselves, but also of our children, our spouses, and others about whom we care. This may not be true in all cases, but obviously it is in some. For this very reason, some older Latter-day Saints are hesitant to work in the ward nursery or Primary. Grandparents become less tolerant of some of the antics of young, squirming grandchildren. Once while I was in a barber shop, an older man announced to the barber his forthcoming retirement. The barber asked what he intended to do with his time. "I'll tell you one thing I don't plan on doing," he responded. "I don't plan on spending all day and night tending our grandchildren."

The saying is probably true that grandparents are glad to see their grandkids come but equally glad to see them go! The feelings of many grandparents are captured in this humorous verse:

> I've seen the lights of Paris,
> I've seen the lights of Rome;
> But the brightest lights to me
> Are taillights taking grandkids home.

As we become older, we may have to practice greater patience and tolerance in our marriages and toward others we love. The first quality of love mentioned in the scriptures is "long suffering," or patience. The differences that once were small and seemingly insignificant in earlier years of marriage may become magnified with age. So couples in their maturing years may have to work much harder at dealing with differences. This is so not because the differences increase, but because our patience and tolerance may tend to decease. By that point in life, however, we should have the skills and maturity to deal with our differences so that "the last is the best."

DIFFERENCES CAN BE COMPLEMENTARY

Regardless of the sources of differences in marriage, Church leaders have admonished married couples to work diligently to resolve or overcome them when they are divisive. As mentioned in chapter one, President Kimball noted that partners "may be as different as fish and fowl, but because there is a great reason for their understanding of each other, they overlook each others' weaknesses, strengthen themselves, and work together."[14]

Many differences between husbands and wives can actually be beneficial. And some of these differences apparently are God-given. Rather than be threatened or puzzled by our divinely given differences, perhaps we should welcome the unique skills and attributes each of us has to offer in a marital relationship and in a family.

In my own marriage, for example, Susan and I go back and forth on when to be tough and when to be tender with our children. Often it is a simple case of justice versus mercy. Susan tends to be more tender and merciful. I tend, on occasions, to be tougher and to want justice to reign. If our children were to experience only one of these tendencies, they would undoubtedly suffer. But with the balance of toughness and tenderness Susan and I are forced to work out, our children have benefited from exposure to both attributes. Each spouse has skills and attributes that benefit the other. If perceived this way, many differences become blessings rather than burdens. President Kimball noted that differing natures of men and woman can be complementary. He said:

> I have mentioned only a few of the special blessings God gives his daughters in helping them to become like him. His sons have their own special opportunities. And in his wisdom and mercy, *our Father made men and women dependent on each other for the full flowering of their potential.* Because their natures are somewhat different, they can

complement each other; because they are in many ways alike, they can understand each other. *Let neither envy the other for their differences;* let both discern what is superficial and what is beautifully basic in those differences, and act accordingly.[15]

Perhaps we now better understand the biblical insight: "Neither is the man without the woman, neither the woman without the man, in the Lord." (1 Corinthians 11:11.)

SEXUAL DIFFERENCES IN MARRIAGE

The previous chapter identified several gender differences between males and females, including quite a few between the brains of men and women. In this chapter I would like to discuss how similarities and differences between males and females can affect the sexual relationship between a husband and wife. In my counseling with couples, I have always been astonished at how little is known about sexual relations and intimacy. Much of this, I believe, is perpetrated by the media, which frequently portrays an inaccurate, immoral, and misleading view of sex. Because of the great amount of misinformation and ignorance in society among some Latter-day Saints and because of the problems it causes, I will need to be frank at times in discussing this sensitive topic.

SEXUAL SIMILARITIES

While there are numerous pronounced differences between males and females with regard to sexuality, men and women share some basic patterns. William Masters and Virginia Johnson were among the first to note that in sexual relations both males and females experience four phases of erotic response: excitement, plateau, orgasm, and resolution.[1]

Excitement: The first phase is arousal, in which sexual excitement begins. During this phase, breathing usually becomes heavier and blood pressure increases. Most men and some women are stimulated by sight. In addition, for both men and women certain types and durations of touch between the male and female lead to this arousal. While men are generally consistent in what arouses them, women appear to be less consistent. What arouses a woman on one occasion may not necessarily arouse her on another. Furthermore, what arouses one woman may not necessarily arouse another woman.

Plateau: After a period of stimulation, both males and females reach a certain point in which the sexual organs are prepared for orgasm. This phase is called the plateau phase and involves an intensity of feeling preceding release through orgasm.

Orgasm: The release or sensation of orgasm is similar for both male and female and is often considered the most pleasurable of the four phases. The major difference between males and females is that men ejaculate during orgasm and women do not. During the orgasm phase, there are several rhythmic reflex contractions of about .8 seconds each in the pelvic areas of both males and females. In addition, women are physiologically capable of achieving several orgasms during times of intimacy, though quite often they will experience only one and sometimes none.

Resolution: The phase following orgasm is the gradual return to the body's basal state. The refractory time, or interval between orgasms, differs in males and females. Most males must wait twenty to sixty minutes before attaining another erection, after which orgasm is again possible. The refractory time for females is just seconds.

Twelve Stages of Physical Intimacy

In addition to the four phases of erotic response that males and females experience, there are also twelve stages of physical intimacy that men and women go through.[2] Desmond Morris, in his book *Intimate Behaviour*, lists the following initial stages of physical behaviour between a man and a woman:

Initial attraction (experienced during dating or "going out"):

1. Eye to body—noticing the other person's physique and looks.

2. Eye to eye — noticing the face and making eye-to-eye contact.

3. Voice to voice — greeting and talking to each other. Will later include extended conversation.

4. Hand to hand — touching or holding hands, usually the first physical contact. It may range from helping a woman out of a car to expressing attraction or attachment.

5. Arm to shoulder — touching or squeezing a shoulder with a hand. Also includes hugging. Such actions may indicate either close or casual appreciation, attraction, or friendship.

6. Arm to waist — placing a hand on the waist or encircling the waist with an arm, one of the first strong indicators of love or romance.

7. Face to face — placing cheek to cheek, talking intimately, and kissing. Such physical proximity indicates that a couple feel comfortable with each other and are attracted to each other. At this point, sexual desire becomes important in the relationship.

8. Hand to head — stroking the other person's head or hair (an extension of stage seven). A sign of emotional closeness, a couple rarely get to this stage unless they are romantically attracted to each other.

Intense intimacy (reserved for marriage):

A knowledge of the next several stages of sexual intimacy is helpful in at least two ways. First, single Latter-day Saints can know what is unacceptable behavior outside of marriage. If some find that they have violated moral commandments, they can begin the repentance necessary to restore the Spirit to their lives and be accepted by the Lord once more. Second, married couples need to know the basic pattern of creating physical intimacy in their marriages. Physical intimacy and sexual fulfillment are extensions of emotional intimacy.

9. Hand to body — caressing or stroking.

10. Mouth to body — kissing parts of the body besides the lips.

11. Touching below the waist — actions that prepare for intercourse.

12. Sexual intercourse — consummation of physical intimacy.

The initial stages 1–8 continue to be important to wives after marriage and should be a normal part of the husband-wife relationship before proceeding to stages 9–12. The entire sequence seems to be the natural order of sexual response for most women and should not be ignored by husbands. Husbands, on the other hand, tend to place great emphasis on the physical intimacy entailed in stages 9–12. Most husbands do not feel that sexual interaction is completed unless these later stages are experienced. This emphasis should not be ignored by wives.

All twelve stages are important in the natural sexual response between husbands and wives. The fact that men and women place greater emphasis on different stages of physical intimacy should not be a major deterrent if each understands the needs and desires of his or her marriage partner and works toward mutual sexual satisfaction.

DIFFERENCES IN SEXUAL RESPONSE

Having noted the similarities in sexual response in males and females, let's examine some differences. Both men and women can be immediately aroused by experiencing erotic stimuli. However, even though the lubricating fluids are immediately present in the genitalia of both sexes, the sensation does not register immediately in the woman's brain. That is one reason why women are believed to respond to sexual stimuli less readily than males. In *Male and Female Realities*, Joe Tanenbaum proposes an interesting theory for this delay:

> A woman does not always feel aroused at the same time as a man. There is a built-in time lapse between the response of her body and the conscious part of her brain. She is protected by nature from making snap decisions that could result in pregnancy.
>
> That doesn't mean she can't or shouldn't be instantly attracted to a man. . . . What it does mean is that the attraction (or repulsion) she feels may not be purely physical. . . . A number of studies show that a woman is less

likely to experience orgasm during a "one-night-stand" than when she is functioning in the context of a stable, long-term relationship.[3]

Male and Female Created He Them

I believe the biblical declaration that the two human bodies, male and female, were created by God. (See Genesis 1:27.) Apparently the two types of bodies and brains he created are quite different. I also believe that these differences are not generally understood by many husbands and wives during the early stages of marriage. This may be particularly true in how men and women perceive and experience sexual relationships. All God's creations, including the ability of men and women to reproduce, were declared "very good" by him. (Genesis 1:31.) Any differences, therefore, could have a divine origin. What, then, are some of the biological differences between men and women with regard to sexuality? Here are just a few noted by Tanenbaum:[4]

1. Women experience a delayed reaction to erotic stimuli.

2. A man can produce more reproductive cells (sperm) in two seconds than a woman can produce (ovum) in her lifetime.

3. The regulating hormones L.H. (Luteinizing Hormone) and F.S.H. (Follicle Stimulating Hormone) in both men and women determine sex drive. In men, these hormones are constantly present, and sexual desire fluctuates several times during the day. In women, the hormone levels are synchronized with ovulation and monthly menstruation cycles. During ovulation these hormones work together to increase her readiness for sexual relations.

4. A man's sex drive increases after puberty and reaches its greatest height in the late teens or early twenties. He reaches his full reproductive maturity between the ages of nineteen to twenty-four. A woman's sex drive increases very slowly after puberty and doesn't reach its peak until the late twenties, where she remains until her middle forties.

5. For a man, orgasm is part of the reproductive process. For a woman, orgasm is not necessary to conceive. Almost all men

experience orgasm each time they ejaculate. Statistics for the
United States reveal that about 5 to 10 percent of women never
experience orgasm, and another 30 to 40 percent of women
experience it only occasionally.

6. Men report that orgasm is the motivating source of enjoyment during intercourse. Women, however, report that affection, intimacy, and love — and not orgasm — are the primary
sources of enjoyment during intercourse.

7. Women are far more cautious than men about entering
sexual relationships. This may be due in part to the woman's
instinctive awareness of the long-term consequences of sexual
relations. Whereas a man, particularly if he is unprincipled, may
consider only his own, immediate satisfaction, a woman is always
conscious that becoming pregnant is a commitment to bear,
nurse, and care for the child.

Anne Moir and David Jessel also note several additional
differences in sexual attitudes and behaviors between males and
females:

8. Men have high sexual energy levels compared to women.
Much of this is due to testosterone, which is the key sexual
activator for both men and women. The authors note that testosterone is a primary agent in the womb in the formation of the
male brain and that men have as much as twenty times the
amount in their bodies as women. On the other hand, sexual
energy for women is at its peak during the menstrual cycle, when
testosterone is at its highest level.[5]

9. Women respond to senses differently from men. Light may
distract a woman, whereas the dark will lessen the distractions
to her other, more sensitive senses: touch, smell, and hearing.
Women are more responsive to talk and touch than are men
during sexual relations.[6]

10. Sexual gratification is not as important to women as it
is to men. Affection and intimacy are the most common reasons
women give for liking sexual relations. Husbands may assume
that their wives have a need for sexual gratification similar to

men, when, in reality, their wives are primarily seeking affection and intimacy.[7]

11. Men are far more likely to enjoy or desire variety in their sexual relations than women. The authors discuss this difference in male and female perspectives by focusing on one pattern that often occurs:

> The desire for sexual novelty is innate in the male brain. . . . The novelty factor can be seen at work every Christmas in the lingerie department of the stores. The men sheepishly rummage through the sheer and exotic nightwear. . . . The male brain places a high priority on the visual when it comes to arousal. Come the New Year, and the same lingerie counters are thronged with women returning the love tokens. . . . They find them embarrassing, and perhaps a little silly. They may well wish that their men had chosen gifts to reflect the different female sensory priorities — body oils, for instance, to enhance and reflect women's greater sensitivity to touch and smell.[8]

Because of these differences, men and women need to realize why and what appeals to each other. Moir and Jessel conclude that

> it is hard to understand nature's plan in arranging this inherent incompatibility between the two sexes of the species. Maybe if we all felt and thought alike we would soon get bored with each other. *But sex would surely be less of a disaster area if these differences were recognised and understood.* . . .
>
> Male and female attitudes — with their biological rather than social basis — cannot be as easily altered as attitudes which have social roots alone. We can, however, come to terms with the reality of our sexual natures, and those of others, respecting the differences rather than decrying them. . . .
>
> *Knowing how different we are could be the first step in becoming a little less alien from each other.*[9]

IS SEX NATURAL IN MARRIAGE?

Imagine the irony of a phone call I received the same week I was writing this chapter. It was from a distraught LDS husband who said his marriage of several years was about to end. A major contributing factor was the lack of any sexual relationship in their marriage. His wife told him she no longer felt any physical attraction for him, and he was devastated. He said, "Dr. Barlow, I want to ask you a question. Is sex normal in a marriage?"

His question surprised me, but before I could answer, he went on to explain that he and his wife had all but given up the physical aspect of their marriage. His wife told him she could take sex or leave it, and she had almost totally left it! He said he still had sexual feelings for her but found they were becoming a painful area of division between them. Finally he stopped talking and asked what I thought.

I noted that it was not normal for a married couple to have no sexual relationship. I am aware of a few happily married couples who *jointly* decided that there would be little or no sexual intercourse in their marriage. They try to be intimate in other ways. Some of these couples are older, while others have experienced various kinds of illnesses or accidents injuring the back or pelvic areas. Such conditions make sexual intercourse extremely painful if not impossible. Neither the caller nor his wife, however, were in these situations.

The lack of sexual relations in marriage, I noted, could pose a danger to the marriage. As just one example, I recalled for him the admonition given to husbands and wives in 1 Corinthians 7:2–5 to not refrain from sexual interaction too long lest either spouse be tempted to seek gratification elsewhere. Such a couple were unknowingly setting up either or both spouses for an extramarital affair.

I shared with the husband a few of the ideas in this chapter about sexual differences in marriage and the need to accommodate and reconcile them. I finally suggested that they talk to their bishop and also referred them to a marriage counselor I knew in their area. I later sent him two articles that I give out in my classes at BYU. But after I hung up, the question still remained: "Is sex a normal or natural act in marriage?"

We Become What We (or the Media) Think About

For some time after that particular phone call, I wondered how that couple and other LDS couples might arrive at a point in their marriages when they wonder if sex is normal. I have a few suspicions.

I believe in the biblical insight that our thoughts greatly influence our behavior. "For as he thinketh in his heart, so is he." (Proverbs 23:7.) We do, indeed, become what we think about. In that regard, I have a genuine concern about the media's distorted portrayal of marriage, especially considering that some Church members may not realize what they are partially, if not wholly, accepting.

For instance, many contemporary television talk shows feature "guests" who are in conflict or contention with others. Those guests include married couples who have some kind of tough or unusual problem (I suppose the theory is that no one would be interested in seeing happy couples enjoying well-adjusted marriages). I wonder how many people who consistently watch these kinds of television programs begin to believe that marriage is not worth the effort. Would he or she begin to suspect that sexual relations between husband and wife are no longer critical or normal, or that as sick aberrations, those relations are to be flaunted?

Likewise, take a look at references to marital situations in newspapers, newscasts, sitcoms, soap operas, and tabloids. What are the dominant themes noted by the current media? Count the articles or newscasts dealing with rape, incest, child sexual molestation, homosexuality, and family violence, including beatings and even murder. What message is being given about what is "normal" and "common" today? I often ask myself how anyone, young or old, married or single, can retain any positive views of sexuality in marriage after being subjected to a constant barrage of misleading information and questionable role models depicted in print and on the screen.

In my chapter on divorce, I discussed many of the signs of

the times. I truly believe that what we are witnessing on television and elsewhere also fits into those signs. Jesus noted that in the last days many people would be deceived. Many would offend and betray one another. The love of many would "wax cold." (See Matthew 24:10, 12, 24.) Have you seen any of these things demonstrated on TV talk shows?

Paul also noted, "This know also, that in the last days perilous times shall come. For men shall be lovers of their own selves, covetous, boasters, proud, blasphemers, disobedient to parents, unthankful, unholy, *without natural affection,* trucebreakers, false accusers, incontinent [sexually uncontrolled], fierce, despisers of those that are good, traitors, heady, highminded, lovers of pleasure more than lovers of God." (2 Timothy 3:1–4; italics added.) The Apostle's advice seems even more relevant today: "From such turn away." (V. 5.) Perhaps he would now say, "From such, turn it off!"

Paul's warning is insightful. His statement that in the last days men and women will be "without natural affection" implies that there is natural affection between the sexes. Moroni warns, "Wherefore, take heed . . . that ye do not judge that which is evil to be of God, or that which is good and of God to be of the devil." (Moroni 7:14.) I personally believe that sexual interaction has, or should have if it doesn't, a divine nature and purpose in a couple's lives. And I believe that part of the "natural affection" that Paul noted would be lacking includes the sexual relationship between husbands and wives. Our bodies, which God created, have hormones, such as testosterone, and other tendencies that help make husbands and wives physically attracted to each other at various times and circumstances. Men and women share a natural or biological attraction.

An estimated seventy billion children have been born into this world. The vast majority of these children have been born without the help of books, tapes, seminars, afternoon talk-show hosts, educators, religious leaders, or physicians that presume to explain how reproduction is supposed to occur. I mention this merely to suggest, again, that there is a naturalness to sexual relationships that doesn't need a great deal of explanation.

SEXUAL MYTHS

If God has given us natural affection and intimacy in marriage, why do sexual relations seem so complicated today? Maybe part of the problem is that we have become saturated with myths concerning sexuality. It was not until the 1960s that William Masters and Virginia Johnson began their clinical and somewhat controversial study of human sexuality. They noted a great many sexual myths that persisted in society, some more prevalent than others. They singled out two in particular:

> The most unfortunate misconception our culture has assigned to sexual functioning is the assumption, by both men and women, that men by divine guidance and infallible instinct are able to discern exactly what a woman wants sexually and when she wants it. Probably this fallacy has interfered with natural sexual interaction as much as any other single factor. The second most frequently encountered sexual fallacy, and therefore a constant deterrent to effective sexual expression, is the assumption, again by both men and women, that sexual expertise is the man's responsibility.[10]

Pertaining to women who had experienced menopause, Masters and Johnson also observed: "Biologists and behaviorists must aid in dispelling the gross psychosocial misconception that postmenopausal women find little of personal interest in continuing opportunity for effective sexual functioning. We must, in fact, destroy the concept that women in the 50–70-year age group not only have no interest in but also have no facility for active sexual expression. Nothing could be further from the truth than the often-expressed concept that aging women do not maintain a high level of sexual orientation."[11]

Three years later, James McCary identified several common sexual myths, including the following:[12]

• The absence of the hymen proves that a girl is not a virgin.

• Sexual intercourse should be avoided during pregnancy.

• Each individual is allotted just so many sexual experiences; when they are used up, sexual activity is finished for that person.

• Alcohol is a sexual stimulant.

• The total or partial removal of the prostate reduces a man's sexual enjoyment and will ultimately destroy his sexual capabilities.

• Menopause or hysterectomy terminates a woman's sex life.

• Sex desire and ability decrease markedly after the ages of forty to fifty.

• A poor sexual adjustment in marriage inevitably spells its doom.

• If one partner desires sexual relations more often than the other, nothing can be done to make the couple sexually more compatible.

• Something is wrong with women who have strong sex drives, achieve climax easily, and are capable of multiple orgasms. (My article "They Twain Shall Be One," which appeared in the *Ensign,* mentioned the myth that women do not or should not have strong sexual inclinations. Several members of the Church wrote to me with questions that indicate the myth is still being perpetuated.[13])

SEXUAL SELFISHNESS, STINGINESS, OR SHARING

Chapter two discusses how it is virtually impossible for one human being to meet all the needs and expectations of another human being in marriage. A marriage is good if 80 percent of the spouses' needs are met in their relationship. Sometimes when either a husband or wife do not experience sexual satisfaction in the marriage, he or she feels justified in seeking this kind of gratification with someone else.

Latter-day Saints make an important distinction: *They agree to seek sexual fulfillment only with their marriage partners.* In this regard, a Latter-day Saint agrees to "forsake all others." He or she has no option to turn to another person, as is now so commonly done in society, to derive sexual fulfillment. Latter-day revelation reaffirms, "Thou shalt not commit adultery" (D&C 42:24), and commands us to cleave unto our spouses *and to none else* (see D&C 42:22).

In the early 1970s, when I was working on my doctorate in marriage and family relations at Florida State University, I was disturbed to learn that as many as 50 percent of husbands and almost as many wives in the United States were estimated to have a sexual encounter after marriage with someone other than their spouses. Today, estimates are much higher and are comparable or worse in many other "civilized" countries. Couples must be consciously careful not to get caught in the tidal wave of immorality and infidelity sweeping the nations.

Since Latter-day Saints are committed to seek sexual satisfaction *only* with their spouses, they have the obligation to help their marriage partners attain that fulfillment. Either a marriage partner can react with sexual selfishness or stinginess, or he or she can perceive marriage as an opportunity for sexual sharing.

Sexual selfishness: Selfishness is often defined as seeking one's own gain at the expense of others or holding on to something so others cannot share it. The dictionary defines selfishness as being "overly concerned with one's own interests and having little concern for others."[14] A spouse caught up in sexual selfishness participates in sexual experiences with the emphasis on what he or she can get rather than give. Latter-day Saint husbands and wives sometimes fail to realize they have their spouses' sexual well-being under their control to either nurture or ignore. Sexual fulfillment is something that LDS husbands and wives, as committed couples under covenant, can help their spouses attain, focusing on the needs of their partners more than on their own needs.

Sexual stinginess: Sometimes a husband or wife will purposely withhold sexual satisfaction from a husband or wife or will give it sparingly in a routine or mechanical way. A "stingy" person is one who gives "grudgingly, . . . less than is needed — or scanty."[15] Sometimes sex becomes a weapon or commodity one withholds from the other as a means of punishment, retribution, manipulation, or retaliation. All of these are forms of contention and disrupt the unity couples strive for in marriage. As many spouses sadly discover, stingy individuals, regardless of what they have to offer (or not offer), are soon avoided.

Sexual sharing: A husband or wife who wants to avoid sexual selfishness or stinginess can do so by being sensitive to the needs of a spouse, which vary from time to time. Sexual fulfillment could be viewed as a gift that only a spouse can share with a marriage partner. Elsewhere I have written about sexual stewardships entrusted into the care of married couples.[16] Like other stewardships we accept and receive in mortality, there are three elements: (1) agency, (2) diligence, and (3) accountability. Sexual sharing is truly a dimension of marriage to be nurtured and cared for.

GOD COMMANDED HUSBANDS AND WIVES TO HAVE SEX

Reading this section heading may make some readers apprehensive. Others may distort the words to allow for their own selfish motives. But please read on. There are several reasons why I believe God commanded husbands and wives to have sexual relationships in their marriage. For instance, God commanded Adam and Eve to reproduce. (See Genesis 1:28.) The creations of Heavenly Father, which include, I believe, the creative powers of Adam and Eve, were declared "very good." (Genesis 1:31.)

President Spencer W. Kimball once noted major differences that often cause divorce, both in and out of the church: "If you study the divorces, as we have had to do in these past years, you will find there are one, two, three, four reasons. Generally, sex is the first. They did not get along sexually. They may not say that in the court. They may not even tell that to their attorneys, but that is the reason . . . Husband and wife . . . are authorized, in fact they are commanded, to have proper sex when they are properly married for time and eternity."[17]

Sexual relations are, therefore, a divinely designed and sanctioned activity when experienced within the prescribed boundaries of marriage. President Kimball and other Church leaders have taught that the primary or main purpose for sexual relations in marriage is that of reproduction. We participate in a plan that was designed before this world was organized, to help bring other beings into mortality. (See D&C 49:15–17.) The first commandment that God gave — "to multiply and replenish the earth" (Genesis 1:28) — has never been rescinded. Equally important was the commandment, reiterated in latter-day revelation, that the sex act was authorized only in a marital relationship. (See Exodus 20:14; D&C 42:24; 59:6; 66:10.)

But is reproduction, or child birth, the only reason husbands and wives are commanded to have sexual relationships? Are there other reasons why sexual relations are not only sanctioned, but also advocated by Deity? Is it possible that sexual relationships between husband and wife may have mental and physical benefits as well? Following are some other insights into the worth of sexual intimacy in marriage.

The Sexually Well Person

Earlier I noted a phone call from an anxious LDS husband who asked if sexual relations were normal in marriage. I mentioned that I sent him two articles with an LDS perspective on sexuality in marriage. What were the two articles?

One was "The Sexually Well Person," by Dr. Val Mac-Murray, an LDS counselor and therapist. Dr. MacMurray presented a profile of what he believed to be a sexually well person. In the profile Dr. MacMurray used the feminine pronouns *her* and *she* but noted that the concepts apply equally to men. Here is the main part of that article:

> I think to the extent that the sexually well person accepts and appreciates her sexuality, it would become a force that made her relationship with herself, with her spouse, and with her God better, stronger, and more binding. In other words, sexuality would not be an unacknowledged element in a person's life, something she tried to ignore about herself, something that was present but not talked about in the

marriage relationship, or a part of one's life from which God was excluded. It would be prayed over and for. In fact, I am convinced that the dominant attitude of the sexually well person toward her sexuality would be gratitude. . . .

1. The sexually well person would feel gratitude towards her own body for its ability to respond to pleasure. . . . Someone who is grateful for her body will respect and appreciate it. She does not deny it, or ignore it. On the contrary, she pays proper attention to it, and welcomes appropriate opportunities to understand its possibilities and potentialities.

2. The sexually well person would feel gratitude to her husband. The possibility of loving a well-beloved other should be a tremendous source of happiness, especially since it is mingled with the realization that our own fulfillment has been made possible by that same spouse's desire to give pleasure as well as receive it. Related to this, and I think it is fairly obvious, there is a sense of unique bonding created by that sexual union. We break bread with many people. We even share our hopes and fears with many people, though certainly not to equal degrees. Though the idea is losing popularity in the culture and society around us, one of the characteristics of a healthy marriage is its sexual fidelity—the luxuriant certainty that only the two of you know and understand that part of the relationship, that only the two of you share that activity, that pleasure, that learning and loving.

3. The sexually well person would also feel grateful to God, not only for the blessing of a physical body, but for knowing and loving another person, and, in a temple marriage, for the sealing ordinances that make the possibility of that union extend beyond death. In addition, just as sexual activity can enhance our respect and love for our own bodies and can increase our loving knowledge of our spouses, so our sexual activity can increase our love, reverence, and knowledge of our heavenly parents. Obviously much of our mortal probation is designed to help us develop godly attributes by giving us opportunities for growth. . . . Such opportunity to understand godliness occurs in the

cherished privacy of our most intimate relationships as husbands and wives. . . .

If our chief attitudes toward our sexuality were respect,
appreciation, and gratitude instead of fear, guilt, or perhaps
anger, what would we teach ourselves, and our children?
How would we reteach concepts that may have been badly
learned in the first place? And how would we go about
healing some of the wounds left by damaging experiences
that people have had up to this point?

I suspect that we would want to emphasize the holiness
of sexuality and eliminate some of the mysteriousness which
makes it frightening and tempting. It would not be something that separates us from God, but something that links
us to him.[18]

The Normal Functioning of Sex

The second article I sent was a *Deseret News* column I had
written quoting from Roy Welker's book *Preparation for Marriage*,
published by the LDS Department of Education. One section
was titled "The Normal Functioning of Sex," in which three
purposes of sexual expression were noted:

> The question is often asked, "Is there a normal func-
> tioning of sex?" A negative answer would imply misunder-
> standing of the question, lack of appreciation of the purposes
> of sex, or a wilful desire toward sex perversion. *Wherever
> there are normal persons there may be normal sex functioning.*
> Evidently the first such functioning must be that of pro-
> creation. Likely no other means for perpetuating the race
> was ever considered. Did man institute it? No. Then God
> must have done so. This makes it a divine process. Should
> it not be so regarded?
>
> The next normal functioning is that of enhancement of
> personality. God has declared "man is not without the
> woman nor the woman without the man in the Lord." [See
> 1 Corinthians 11:11.] Men and women who have lived
> normally and happily together for years can testify to the
> personality contributions of each to the other in normal
> sex relationship. Those who have failed can testify to the
> personality deterioration they have suffered.

In the previous section mention was made of spiritual values stimulated by the single standard. Another normal function of sex is that of spiritual unfoldment. This is a natural conclusion of personality enhancement and of thoughtful and purposeful procreation. A sane approach to the subject can find no other conclusion. *All the enduring values of life are heightened, taking on an added significance, when sex functions in its normal ways.*[19]

6

BRENT AND SUSAN'S DIFFERENCES

Much of my interest in writing this book has come from the experiences Susan and I have had in dealing with the differences that have emerged or have been discovered in our marriage. Like many other young couples in love, Susan and I were not aware of or, for that matter, really did not care about any differences we might have had. (Romantic love seems to nullify pragmaticism.) Luckily, the many differences we have discovered are not truly major ones. But there are several minor but significant differences that we have had to deal with in our twenty-eight years of marriage. Let me share just a few with you.

SHOPPING

For me, shopping with Susan is the closest thing to death without actually dying. Susan likes to shop. For her it is therapeutic. She likes to look at things and hunt for bargains. When I go shopping, I have a very simple strategy: (1) find what I want to buy, (2) buy it, and (3) get out of the store. What I pay for the item is less important than how fast I can find it and leave. If a clerk or sales person can help me speed up the process, so much the better. But my wife likes to "look around" and compare one item with another. Let me give you an example of what I mean.

One time when I needed a new pair of shoes, I went to the University Mall in Orem, walked in a shoe store, and within a few minutes picked out a pair that I liked. I was about to buy them but decided that I had better get Susan's input on the shoes before making the purchase. So I went home and invited her to return to the mall with me to buy a pair of shoes. She obliged.

Later that afternoon we went back to that same shoe store, and I showed her the ones that I liked. She liked them too. "Good," I said, "let's buy them and leave."

My wife said something like "No, that's not the way you buy shoes." She then asked the shoe salesman, "Do you have any other shoes?"

I answered her question for her. "Sure, he has other shoes. Just look around. They're all over the store."

Susan nodded to the salesman. "We would like to see some other shoes."

"Why?" I asked. There was no response. The salesman started carrying out other pairs of shoes from the back room. We looked at several more pairs, and I even tried a few of them on. A short time later my wife turned to the clerk and said, "Thanks. We'll be back."

"Where are we going?" I muttered as I tied the laces in my old pair of shoes.

"Follow me," Susan instructed.

So where do you think we went? I followed her to several other shoe stores in the mall and tried on other shoes similar to the first pair I liked at the first shoe store. After what seemed like endless hours of looking at and trying on shoes, Susan said, "Come with me."

Again I asked the foolish question, "Where are we going?" And where do you think we went? To the first shoe store, where we bought the first pair of shoes that I liked.

After we paid the clerk, Susan said, "There, that's how you shop for shoes!"

PILLOWS

We recently bought a new bedspread for the bed in our master bedroom. It looked very nice. One night Susan said, "I think we should get some new pillows to put on our bed for decorations. What do you think?"

I naïvely agreed. One or two small frilly pillows on her side of the bed shouldn't mess up my macho side of the bed too much. The next day Susan went shopping for pillows.

Imagine my shock that night when I decided to go to bed. I walked in the bedroom and what did I find? Not one. Not two. But *six* pillows artistically placed on our bed. And they were not all small pillows. Two of them were about three feet long!

Susan came in the room to go to bed, and I muttered something about not understanding the need for six pillows on the bed and how I'd have to go to bed twenty minutes early to get all the pillows off so I could sleep. Then I made an observation that, despite being used often, has never gotten me anywhere in dealing with differences in our marriage: "None of my friends I know of have six pillows on their bed."

Susan made her standard reply, from which she gets great mileage: "All my friends I know of have six *or more* pillows on their bed."

TOURIST ACTIVITIES

A few years ago Susan and I flew to Hawaii for a series of lectures I was to give for BYU's Know Your Religion program. While in the Hawaiian Islands, I was to speak to about seven stakes in ten days, plus give the devotional speech at the BYU-Hawaii campus.

We arrived in Kona on the Big Island and had a few hours before I had to speak. On the flight over I had thumbed through many pictures of the Hawaiian scenery, so I picked up the keys to our rental car and suggested we go sight-seeing before speaking that evening.

Susan hesitated. She said she couldn't wait to go to the tourist shops we had seen on the way to the motel. As we discussed our desires in greater detail, our differences became more evident and pronounced. Would we go driving or shopping that afternoon?

"Driving!" I insisted.

"Shopping," Susan countered.

"Driving!"

"Shopping!"

"Driving!"

"Shopping!"

I indicated she was being obstinate and self-centered. She suggested the possibility that we were both in love with the same man.

So what did we do that afternoon in Kona? All I can say is we bought a lot of souvenirs and things to take home to the children. Susan saw no problem since she said everything she purchased was on sale. She even pointed out how much money we had saved by only purchasing on-sale items.

FOOD AND DRINK

I remember an experience we had shortly after we were married. While we were watching television one night, I decided to go to the refrigerator to get some tomato juice. I asked Susan if she would like some too. I returned a few minutes later and handed Susan her glass of tomato juice. She took one small taste and made a funny face.

"This tomato juice tastes like it has salt in it," she stated.

I had no problem with that observation. "Sure it tastes salty. I put salt in it."

"Why?" she asked

"Everyone I know puts salt in tomato juice," I observed with keen insight.

"No one I know puts salt in tomato juice," Susan rejoined.

Then followed what seemed like a two-hour debate on whether tomatoes were a vegetable or a fruit and consequently whether they required salt or sugar for seasoning. It was one of those discussions that go nowhere, like the ones that arise by asking, "If I died, would you marry again?" Or, "if you could change just one thing about me, what would that be?" Those discussions are like jogging in quicksand. You just sink deeper and deeper until you are in so deep you can't get out.

Whether or not you put salt in tomato juice was just my first introduction to a multitude of differences in dealing with foods. Being from California, Susan introduced me to avocado sandwiches . . . once! Have you ever seen an avocado sandwich? And being from Sanpete County, I introduced my wife to catsup. We could probably prove our true love for each other by both of us eating avocado sandwiches covered with catsup. But our love hasn't matured to that level . . . yet.

And imagine my shock the first time Susan made scrambled eggs for breakfast. They looked and tasted different. Much to my surprise, I discovered she had mixed in milk when scrambling the eggs — and she didn't even deny it. She said her mother had always mixed milk with scrambled eggs, and I replied that mine never had. I suggested that if Providence had intended milk to be mixed with eggs that somewhere along the line a cow would have been crossed with a chicken. The argument didn't hold. I have since discovered that there are few purists left in this world who eat scrambled eggs without milk. To this day in the Barlow home, we still have scrambled eggs mixed with milk. That is, until I am home alone and can finally make scrambled eggs the proper way — without milk.

ENERGY LEVELS

If you were to follow Susan and me around for a few days, you would note that our energy levels peak at different times. Basically, I am a morning person. Susan is a night person. About 10:45 P.M. each night I start falling asleep. By 11:00 P.M. I am out . . . cold. You can set your watch by it. Susan, on the other hand, is just picking up steam by the time the 10:00 P.M. news comes on television. Some of her best work and most creative efforts are done between ten and midnight.

In the morning, however, something quite different occurs. I am awake by 5:00 or 5:30 each morning. By then Susan is just midway through her night's rest. And when I wake up, I wake up all at once. So I get out of bed. My wife, on the other hand, wakes up one limb at a time.

Not that differing energy levels make that much difference in our marriage. But they do create some interesting situations. For instance, when we take our children to Lagoon (Utah's version of Disneyland) or some similar place for recreation, I am dead tired by the time we pull in the driveway that night. It seems as though I crawl from the car to the front door. Susan, on the other hand, appears to be full of vim and vigor as we (and the kids never seem to include themselves in that *we*) proceed to unpack the car.

Go on a long drive, however, and that is a different story. If we are driving to Southern California, Susan is asleep by the time we reach Payson. Two or three times during the fifteen-hour ride she seems to come out of her etherlike trance and asks something about me wanting her to drive. Before I can say yes, she has fallen back asleep, so I proceed on.

About sixty miles from our destination in California, however, something miraculous happens. She becomes readily awake and volunteers to drive "the rest of the way." By that time I am so tired from fourteen hours of driving that I gladly accept. So she completes that last hour of the trip. We arrive at our destination with her looking fresh and relaxed and me passed out with exhaustion, my head tilted back and my mouth open (much to the delight of our children and other curious onlookers when we arrive). Is there any justice in life at all?

TEMPERATURE REACTIONS

This is one of the differences we discovered two days after we were married. We went to the Grand Canyon on our honeymoon, and the second day of our travel we were somewhere in Arizona late one afternoon riding along in our 1963 Corvair, which was then two years old. As we rode along I began to perspire, so I did the logical thing. I reached over and turned on the air conditioner. We had not driven more than two miles when Susan reached over and nonchalantly turned the air conditioner off. We drove a few more miles with me sweating, so I reached over and turned on the air conditioning once again, much to my relief. I won't even need to tell you her next move.

After several switches of the air conditioning, we had a "friendly conversation." I said, "It's hot." Susan said, "It's just right." I wondered what was wrong with my new sweet bride of some forty-eight hours. *Anyone* could tell it was hot. But not Susan. She felt just right. It took us only two days to discover a difference that has persisted during our entire marriage and that will likely continue on into eternity. (I hope the resurrection takes care of part of this.) I, like so many men, feel more comfortable in cooler temperatures. Susan, I later found out, is more comfortable in warmer temperatures.

What happened with the air conditioner on our Corvair has continued with the thermostat to our furnace in the winter and air conditioner in the summer. For several years we have had lively discussions on whether a particular day, room, or climate is really warm or cold. I have been convinced of my keen insight. She has been convinced of the superiority of hers. Neither of us has budged. So finally we bought a thermometer we carry around from room to room. It is very precise and accurate. But we have not yet been able to agree on what is, for me, "too hot." For her, anything under 75 degrees is too cold. For me, the upper seventies begin to get too warm.

RELIGION

Even though Susan and I were both brought up in active LDS homes, we discovered soon after we were married that we had some differences on how to "live our religion." What was appropriate Sunday activity? Would we allow nonmember friends to smoke or drink coffee in our home? How often and where should we pray? Should we pray over our food before eating in a restaurant? How long does Fast Sunday actually last? And when does it begin? Then there was tithing.

Susan had been taught that immediately after she received money or a check from work, she should take her tithing to the bishop the following Sunday. I had always paid tithing but figured I had until December 31 to get it in. The Lord only counts once a year, so I believed.

Just a few months after we were married, we had the opportunity to buy half a beef. The only money we had to pay for it was our tithing for that month. I had a National Guard check coming in the next few weeks, and I suggested we could catch up on our tithing then. I talked her into buying the beef with tithing money, but do you think she would let me enjoy it? Susan would cook some steaks and then call, "Come and eat the Lord's beef." How and when to pay tithing was a minor difference we encountered, which has since been resolved. I soon came around to Susan's point of view, and we have since paid our tithing immediately.

MAKING DECISIONS

When we married, we really didn't have any mechanism in place for making decisions. I wanted her to go along with my ideas, and she wanted me to accept hers. We tried to figure out a good way to go about making decisions.

I kept reading Ephesians 5:22 over and over to Susan, "Wives, submit yourselves unto your own husbands," but somehow she didn't interpret the scripture the way I did. She wanted me to read the verses that followed, which say that a husband is supposed to love his wife enough to give his life for her.

Finally we decided that I, as "head of the home," would make all the major decisions, and she would make the minor ones. That seemed fair to me in my youthful ignorance as a new husband. All I can say is that after twenty-eight years of marriage, there have been few "major" decisions to make. Susan believes they all have been minor ones and acts according to our agreement.

PARENTING

Rearing our children takes first place as the area in which Susan and I differ most. Part of this is due to our families of origin. She was brought up as an only child, and I grew up with two sisters. As might be expected, her parents differed somewhat from mine regarding child rearing. Not that one was more correct than the other, they just approached the task differently. Because of this and because of our individual personalities and attitudes, Susan and I differ sometimes in what to do with our children.

When should we be tough? And when should we be tender? Do we both share the responsibility for discipline, or is that the father's job? What activities should our children engage in with peers and when? What actually constitutes a date? Can an LDS teenager go on a date three weeks before his or her sixteenth birthday? Who decides when children can not or should not do a particular thing? And who should inform them of the decision? The list seems to go on and on. In hindsight, I am amazed that there have been more areas of agreement than disagreement in rearing our children. But we are not through with parenting yet!

PERCEPTION OF TIME AND SPACE

We quickly realized that we differed in how we deal with time and space. For instance, the first time we were going somewhere for the evening, Susan said, "I'll be ready in ten minutes." Fair enough. So I sat down on the couch (actually I paced the floor) and waited for the ten minutes to end. When the ten minutes ended, so did my patience. I found out that "ten minutes" is a general term that has specific meaning to me but relatively none to her. She'll leave the house at seven P.M. to "run to the store for a half hour" and return at nine. In addition, I like to get to church not only on time, but ten minutes early. If she is in the building when the bishop greets the congregation, we are, in her way of thinking, "on time."

As to space, I will "load" the dishwasher until no more dishes can fit in. I really believe that. But Susan comes in and loads half a sinkful more. How she fits them in, I'll never know. The space difference also extends to place. When we go somewhere, I like directions, a map, or at least an address. If Susan has been there, no big deal. "Just drive down to the 7–Eleven and turn left," she'll say, "and then I'll direct you from there." She will have me drive up and down a few streets so she can recognize the house. Really, I would prefer an exact address. But she likes to rove.

THROWERS AND SAVERS

Susan is a thrower and I am a saver, at least when it comes to my things. She cannot understand the emotional attachment I have to my army boots, which are stored in the garage. After I was discharged from the National Guard, I wanted to keep them, "in case I was called up again." That was twenty-five years ago. Who knows? I may need my army boots again. Susan wants to throw them out.

But with her things, the reverse is true — Susan becomes the saver and I am the thrower. Her sewing room, for example, has patterns left over from Civil War times. Or there are the recipes in various places around the house. She saves recipes she has never used and likely never will. She has boxes and boxes of them on various shelves. I say "throw them out," but she thinks she needs them.

In spite of all these differences and others, and some additional ones that likely will emerge in the future (and I haven't the slightest notion of what they will be), Susan and I are still in love, more so now than we were on our wedding day. And we remain very committed to each other, our marriage, and our children. But still, we have had to learn to deal with our differences. And so will you in your marriage. How can this be done? Several suggestions are given in the chapters that follow.

WAYS TO DEAL WITH DIFFERENCES IN MARRIAGE

7

IDENTIFYING YOUR DIFFERENCES

In chapter six I shared with you several differences that have emerged in my marriage. Some of these, Susan and I recognized immediately. With others, one or both of us had to acknowledge the differences as legitimate (getting out of the I'm-right-you're-wrong syndrome). And still others, we realized only after consciously trying to identify some things we couldn't quite put our fingers on at first. The point is, before we can work on reconciling our differences, we must first know what they are. Quite a few of them may be minor, which we can just choose not to let bother us, and a number of them may be major, requiring a couple's joint efforts to reconcile them. Differences must be identified and acknowledged by both husband and wife before they can be dealt with.

Before you begin to identify your differences, you may want to go to your local library or Christian book store and obtain a copy of *Incompatibility: Grounds for a Great Marriage,* by Chuck and Barb Snyder. The Snyders claim to be the world's most opposite couple, and chapter one of their book lists over fifty differences they had identified at a time when they were seriously considering divorce. Here are some of the differences they noted:[1]

She likes butter. He likes margarine.

She is a low-energy person. He is a high-energy person.

She is relationship-oriented. He is goal-oriented.

She is left-handed. He is right-handed.

She is practical. He is a dreamer.

She likes the toilet paper roll to roll toward her. He doesn't care which way it rolls.

She likes to listen to soft violin music. He likes to listen to loud country music.

She has a difficult time making decisions. He makes them easily.

She likes a variety of foods. He likes the same old standbys.

She came from a loud family in which everyone shouted at each other. He came from a quiet family in which hardly anyone ever raised a voice.

She wants to resolve conflict immediately. He wants to wait awhile.

She wants to talk when she is angry. He doesn't want to talk when either of them is angry.

She believes stoplights are ordained of God to bring order into our lives. He believes stoplights are tools of Satan to disrupt his life.

She is a perfectionist. He is disorderly.

She keeps a clean desk. He has a roll top.

She likes one or two pets. He likes several.

She is a saver. He is a spender.

She is a planner. He is impulsive.

She asks for directions when she gets lost. He feels that asking for directions is a sign of weakness.

She feels comfortable taking things back to the store when they aren't exactly what she wants. He stores them in the garage.

She likes to take her time. He is always in a hurry.

She does one thing at a time to conclusion. He likes to do many things at once.

She hates paperwork. He handles paperwork easily.

She smashes bugs in the house and kills spiders. He carefully takes them outside to safety.

Despite a multitude of differences and a marriage that seemed doomed, this Christian couple were able to avoid separation and deal successfully with their differences. They attribute much of their success to their Christian faith and their relationship with Jesus Christ.

Just a note of caution before you begin to identify your differences. I suggest that you do not do this exercise right after the honeymoon or during the first six months of the marriage. Enjoy the wedded bliss! Research has noted that most married couples continue the high phase of romance well into the first six months of marriage. It is usually during the last half of the first year that differences become more pronounced and noticeable. President Spencer W. Kimball has remarked:

> Two people coming from different backgrounds soon learn after the ceremony is performed that stark reality must be faced. There is no longer a life of fantasy or of make-believe; we must come out of the clouds and put our feet firmly on the earth. Responsibility must be assumed and new duties must be accepted. Some personal freedoms must be relinquished and many adjustments, unselfish adjustments, must be made.
>
> One comes to realize very soon after marriage that the spouse has weaknesses not previously revealed nor discovered. The virtues which were constantly magnified during courtship now grow relatively smaller, and the weaknesses which seemed so small and insignificant during courtship now grow to sizeable proportions. The hour has come for understanding hearts, for self-appraisal, and for good common sense, reasoning, and planning.[2]

If you have recently married, skip the following exercise for a few months and just get used to living together. Come back to it later. I might add, however, that identifying differences may be an excellent exercise to complete for couples who are considering marriage. Couples may identify differences during this stage of the relationship that may have to be dealt with before the marriage, such as how many children each partner wants or how involved each person wants to be in church activity after marriage. Couples happily married for extended periods of time have two options: (1) They can ignore the differences, choosing to live with them (see chapter ten on coexistence) or (2) they can identify their differences and learn to deal with them.

EXERCISE FOR IDENTIFYING YOUR DIFFERENCES

Step 1. On a sheet of paper, list the differences that exist between you and your spouse. The differences do not have to be in any particular order, nor do they have to be listed in priority of importance. Just jot them down. Perhaps you have some of the ones Susan and I have identified in chapter six or some of those mentioned by Chuck and Barb Snyder.

Step 2. After you have listed your differences, contemplate the following quotation from Elder B. H. Roberts: "In essentials let there be unity; in non-essentials, liberty; and in all things, charity!"[3] The phrase suggests that in "essentials"—things that really matter—there must be some degree of unity. In nonessentials—things of lesser importance—we should exercise great tolerance and liberty. And in all cases in dealing with differences, we should act with kindness, love, or charity.

Step 3. Now, go through the list you have made and identify each difference as either an *essential* difference or a *nonessential* difference.

Essential Differences

Some differences are "core symbols" in a marital relationship; that is, they represent some things that are central or "core" in matters of importance. For example, one core symbol might be the couple's differences with money management. Perhaps either husband or wife (or both!) fail to keep track of money spent or bills owed. Inability to manage money typically affects more than a couple's credit rating. It often has a detrimental impact on the marriage relationship and directly affects the couple's ability to provide for themselves and their family.

Some differences that would normally be incidental could become core symbols. For instance, differences in personal hygiene—how often a person shampoos, what brand of toothpaste he or she prefers, and so on—are relatively unimportant. But they would become critical if perhaps one spouse failed to bathe often, so that the body odor became offensive to the other spouse and others around them. Differences in standards of personal cleanliness could become an important issue in a marriage.

Essential differences, then, are those rather serious areas, large or small, that cause constant concern, hurt, and irritation in a marriage. If left unattended or unresolved, they may lead to marital disruption and possibly divorce.

Nonessential Differences

Every marriage has differences that are not serious but are nevertheless areas of concern and disagreement. The concern or irritation may be over clothes left on the floor, differences in food preferences or eating habits, or speech mannerisms. There are such frequently noted differences as squeezing the toothpaste tube from the middle or end or having the toilet paper roll forward or backward. And how about the butter? Should it be kept in the cupboard or in the refrigerator?

One of the most humorous experiences I ever had took place in a class of young married couples at BYU. One day we were discussing the differences they had discovered. I asked the class to name some, and four young wives immediately raised their hands. One of them stated, "I can't stand it when I walk into the bathroom and my husband has left the toilet seat up!" Everyone laughed, but the other three young women had raised their hands to say the same thing. For these four young women, toilet seats up was an essential difference. All the husbands in the class thought it was a nonessential. So I was able to teach them one critical point: If something, such as the position of the toilet seat, is an essential difference for one, it should also be considered an essential difference for the other. Most of the young husbands left the class having committed to keep the toilet seats down in their apartments. What is humorous and nonessential to one can be serious and essential to the other.

After you have completed the exercise to identify your differences, you should have a list in which each entry is tagged with the word *essential* or *nonessential*. Most groups in which I have conducted this exercise label a high percentage (90 percent or higher) of the differences as nonessential. The differences may cause concern and be irritating, but they are not issues or areas that could threaten to overthrow the marriage. With almost every couple, however, there are a few, perhaps only one or two, differences identified as essential, which means they cause more concern, or even pain, and disrupt the marriage. In some cases, the differences, if left unattended, could possibly lead to divorce.

Now that you have acknowledged and categorized your differences into two groups, you are ready to proceed to the most important part of this book. The next five chapters discuss ways to deal with both essential and nonessential differences. As you work through your differences, remember this one important idea: Start with the smallest difference, the one with the least emotional impact. Save the big ones for last, after you have gained a few skills and insights in dealing with differences. Don't try and jump a four-foot wall when you have only three-foot skills! Give yourself and your spouse some time to work through the differences and try to keep your sense of humor during the process.

One nonessential for me when Susan and I married was hair spray. Susan would buy cans of hair spray and spray deodorant that looked exactly alike and put them next to each other on the shelf. I still remember the sensation of getting up in the morning, showering, and then, with my glasses still off, grabbing an aerosol can and spraying my arm pits with hair spray. We finally worked through that one by collaboration. (See chapter ten.) Susan kept her two cans of spray where she wanted, and I got my own smaller can of "men's deodorant" and put it where I wanted. We kept a nonessential difference from becoming an essential difference. (I can imagine the newspaper headline if we hadn't resolved that difference: "BYU Marriage Counselor and Wife Divorce after Long-standing Dispute over Hair Spray!")

THE CHANGE-FIRST PRINCIPLE

When discussing differences, many husbands and wives are anxious to document the weaknesses of their partners and to present plenty of suggestions on ways *their spouses* can change. But I would like to discuss with you a vital principle called the change-first principle, where the emphasis for change begins with you, not your marriage partner.[1]

There are two near-universal responses in human behavior that occur when people have allowed their differences to develop into conflict: (1) it's always the other person's fault, and (2) a person will change only after the other decides to change or "give in." Responsibility for the cause of the problem or the need to change is almost always assigned to the other person. Few of us have the capacity or even the desire to look at our own behavior objectively, to see what part we may have in either the origin of or the solution to the problem. This is true with regard to relationships between governments, business associates, neighbors, friends, and roommates. It sometimes even occurs in the Church among members and between missionary companions.

This phenomenon is particularly evident in contemporary marital relationships. When trouble, conflict, or problems occur in marriage, the human tendency is to blame our marriage partners first. We often refuse to make any initial efforts to change until our spouses acknowledge the errors or "evils" of their ways (with the help of our incessant promptings). We say or think things like "If only he would . . . " or "If only she could . . . ," and then we list, mentally or out loud, all the changes that we perceive our spouses need to make to improve the marriage. We tend to ignore or overlook our own shortcomings or need for change.

In the Sermon on the Mount, the Savior gave one of the greatest insights into this human tendency when he taught what is sometimes called the change-first principle. He said, "Why beholdest thou the mote that is in thy brother's [or spouse's] eye, but considerest not the beam that is in thine own eye? Or how wilt thou say to thy brother [or spouse], Let me pull out the mote out of thine eye; and, behold, a beam is in thine own eye? Thou hypocrite, first cast out the beam out of thine own eye; and then shalt thou see clearly to cast out the mote out of thy brother's [or spouse's] eye." (Matthew 7:3–5.)

As a carpenter, Jesus knew that a beam was a large, long piece of wood and that a mote was a small speck of sawdust. Through this comparison, he asked his disciples, including husbands and wives, why they were so skilled in perceiving the small inadequacies in others and yet were oblivious or nearly blinded to their own larger imperfections. Jesus admonished them to seek to cast out, or overcome, their own larger imperfections and to be less inclined to try to change someone else's smaller inadequacies — in other words, to change first.

Today, professionals in human behavior give similar advice to married couples. A husband and wife who love each other will try to make small, reasonable changes in their relationship so their marriage will be more stable and satisfying. But there is danger in equating the willingness of another to change with his or her love and commitment to the marriage. In fact, in their book *Husbands and Wives: The Guide for Men and Women Who Want to Stay Married,* two psychologists, Dr. Melvyn Kinder and Dr. Connell Cowan, claim that it is a fallacy to believe that your mate should change for you if he or she really loves you. They note:

Couples sometimes go on trying to change each other long after it is clear that it won't work. What happens is that the one who wants change begins to build a case that gets increasingly extreme and dramatic, even obsessional, as though the validity of the marriage hinged on some specific change. Getting a spouse to change becomes tantamount to getting him or her to love you.

You are allowing yourself to [equate change with love] whenever you find yourself being unrelenting in your effort to persuade your spouse to be different. Some of the clues are constant criticism, nagging, and at times uncontrolled irritability when your mate's awful and unwanted behavior manifests itself. Again, love is about acceptance. Your mate can love you and still find it nearly impossible to modify his or her behavior in any lasting and consistent way.[2]

The changes in marriage referred to in this chapter are changes in normal day-to-day behaviors common to most marital relationships. Some changes in a marriage partner may be necessary, on occasion, when the behavior is the kind that should not be tolerated, negotiated, or compromised. Such behaviors include repeated infidelity, dishonesty, mental and physical abuse, substance (drug) abuse, prolonged neglect, and illegal activities. (See chapter eleven on confrontation.) Otherwise, our marriages would benefit far more by applying the change-first principle than by insisting on change in our partners.

Closely related to the change-first principle, I believe, is the law of the harvest, which likewise emphasizes the importance and consequences of individual efforts. The law of the harvest is simply "we reap what we sow." (See Galatians 6:7.) The idea has annoyed spouses who are unhappily married because it suggests that, no matter what, they are partly responsible for what is happening in the marriage. Some people also misconstrue the law of the harvest to mean that every bad or good thing that happens to them is the result of something they have done. Neither of these assumptions is true. Rather, the law says that what we do has consequences. Married individuals may not have been instrumental in sowing the seeds of discord, unhappiness, or disharmony, but they may have helped nurture the growth of seeds of discord and mistrust. That is the negative aspect of the law of the harvest.

There is a positive side to the law of the harvest: if you want a better relationship with your spouse, change first. You plant the seeds of harmony, trust, and love, and then nurture the seedlings long enough for them to grow and bear fruit. The promise is that eventually you will reap what you sow. Some couples in troubled marriages or families may be hesitant or even fearful to try if previous efforts have been unsuccessful. Will the process really work if renewed efforts are made once again? The law of the harvest was reiterated in latter-day revelation. It states, "Fear not to do good, . . . for whatsoever ye sow, that shall ye also reap; therefore, if ye sow good ye shall also reap good for your reward. Therefore, fear not, little flock; do good." (D&C 6:33–34.)

Another law related to the change-first principle and the law of the harvest is the law of the boomerang, or "what goes out comes back." In other words, how we treat others generally becomes the way they treat us. (If you want to test this "law" in the negative sense, go out in the woods and kick a skunk!) In the Sermon on the Mount, Jesus admonished, "All things whatsoever ye would that men should do to you, do ye even so to them." (Matthew 7:12.) Commonly called the Golden Rule, this teaching urges us to treat others the way we would like to be treated. This advice, given two millennia ago, is still timely for married couples. According to the law of the boomerang, then, our spouses will eventually treat us better as we treat them better.

The law of the boomerang is taught in at least three other scriptures. Alma cautioned his son, Corianton, about his previous questionable conduct and noted, "For that which ye do send out shall return unto you again." (Alma 41:15.) In Ecclesiastes we read, "Cast thy bread upon the waters: for thou shalt find it after many days." (11:1.) The Savior taught, "Give, and it shall be given unto you; good measure, pressed down, and shaken together, and running over, shall men give into your bosom. For with the same measure that ye mete withal it shall be measured to you again." (Luke 6:38.)

These three concepts, the change-first principle, the law of the harvest, and the law of the boomerang are all taught in the scriptures and seem to emphasize the importance of individual efforts and consequences. Once we have learned that we really can't change another person, we can then focus on what changes are needed in our own lives. Can you imagine what would happen to marriages if we each took the initiative and bore the responsibility to get our own lives in order before making a single request or demand of our spouses? If that were so, I expect that by the time we got around to making our requests, there would be few left to be made.

If you want to change your marriage, get a mirror rather than a microscope. Start with yourself and ask this key question: "What would it be like to be married to me?" What if your spouse were exactly like you? What would he or she be like to live with? Start there! What changes could you make in your life right now to make yourself easier to live with and your marriage more tolerable for your spouse?

Another way to discover what changes you may need to make is simply to ask the Lord: "Ask, and it shall be given you." (Matthew 7:7.) The Lord has promised that "if men [and women] come unto me I will show unto them their weakness. . . . For if they humble themselves before me, and have faith in me, then will I make weak things become strong unto them." (Ether 12:27.)

In one priesthood meeting, I taught a lesson on husband and wife relationships and asked the brethren how many would like to receive a revelation. Every hand went up. I then suggested that we all go home and ask our wives how we could be better husbands. (I should add that I followed my own advice and had a very informative discussion with Susan for more than an hour that afternoon!)

Every marriage counselor has to make an assessment during

the initial meeting with a couple. Does he or she strengthen the individuals by working on the marriage? Or strengthen the marriage by stabilizing the individual lives? Actually, the process is cyclical. Both need to be done. But where to begin? After many years of counseling, I have realized a simple truth: *Stable men and women make stable marriages!* By helping individuals get their lives in order, counselors help most marriages improve. The initial obstacle to this is that most spouses usually think that their partners are the ones who need help in stabilizing.

FOUR AREAS OF INDIVIDUAL CHANGE

What would happen in marriages today if all husbands and wives decided to stabilize *their own lives?* What if all of us decided to change first in four important areas of our lives: (1) physical, (2) mental, (3) social, and (4) spiritual?

Physical Word of Wisdom

When a spouse experiences ill health or another kind of physical problem, adjustments may often have to be made in the marriage. The problem may result from the natural process of aging. Others may occur from abusing the body with alcohol, tobacco, tea, or coffee. Unwise use of drugs, prescribed and otherwise, can alter moods or physical functioning and contribute to marital discord. Lack of sleep can also cause physical problems and affect the marriage.

Not surprisingly then, the Lord has given us a number of guidelines relating to our physical lives, guidelines that might be called a physical Word of Wisdom. He has admonished us to get needed rest: "Retire to thy bed early, that ye may not be weary; arise early, that your bodies and your minds may be invigorated." (D&C 88:124) He has counseled us on proper nutrition (see D&C 89:10–16) and encouraged us to get adequate exercise so that we "shall run and not be weary, and shall walk and not faint." (V. 20.) Many husbands and wives note vast improvements in their marriages when they take better care of their own physical health.

Mental Word of Wisdom

Perhaps there is also a need for a mental Word of Wisdom. Wise men and women know the importance of balance in life. In his discourse, King Benjamin noted that "it is not requisite that a man should run faster than he has strength." (Mosiah 4:27.) In the latter days the Prophet Joseph Smith had a monumental work to perform, which required great physical and emotional strength. Similarly, he was admonished, "Do not run faster or labor more than you have strength and means." (D&C 10:4.) Apparently Joseph learned how to relax and unwind on occasion as the need arose. One associate noted, "At that time Joseph was studying Greek and Latin, and when he got tired studying he would go and play with the children in their games about the house, to give himself exercise. Then he would go back to his studies as before."[3]

Another associate recalled that Joseph "was preaching once, and he said it tried some of the pious folks to see him play ball with the boys. He then related a story of a certain prophet who was sitting under the shade of a tree amusing himself in some way, when a hunter came along with his bow and arrow, and reproved him. The prophet asked him if he kept his bow strung up all the time. The hunter answered that he did not. The prophet asked why, and he said it would lose its elasticity if he did. The prophet said it was just so with his mind, he did not want it strung up all the time."[4]

It is interesting to note that in June 1850, just three years after the pioneers arrived in Salt Lake Valley, the first theatrical play was given in the Bowery on Temple Square. President Brigham Young placed great emphasis on drama, literature, the arts, music, singing, and dancing (see D&C 136:28) during those early and difficult years of conquering the Western deserts. Why? Two of his daughters later related this teaching of Brigham Young: "Life is best enjoyed when time periods are evenly divided between labour, sleep and recreation. All men, women and children should labour; all must sleep; and if mental and physical balance is to be maintained, all people should spend one-third of their time in recreation which is rebuilding, voluntary activity — never idleness. 'Eight hours work, eight hours sleep, and eight hours recreation' was Brigham Young's motto. *Re-creation* is indeed the meaning of recreation."[5]

Today, as anciently, "to every thing there is a season, and a time to every purpose under the heaven: . . . a time to laugh; . . . and a time to dance." (Ecclesiastes 3:1, 4.)

A Social Word of Wisdom

A social Word of Wisdom would suggest that we learn to live peaceably with our neighbors, extended family members, associates, and friends. In the marriages that seem to function best in today's society, husbands and wives enjoy interaction with a well-established support network of people. When they need to, a couple can turn to that network for emotional and social support. A social Word of Wisdom would include leaving father and mother and yet honoring them. (See Genesis 2:24; Exodus 20:12.)

It would also include learning and practicing the gospel principle of long-suffering, or patience, which is the first quality of pure love mentioned in the scriptures. (See 1 Corinthians 13:4; Moroni 7:45.) We would learn and practice forgiveness (see Matthew 6:12, 14–15; Luke 17:3–4; D&C 64:8–10) and reconciliation (see Matthew 5:23–25; 18:15) with neighbors, family members, friends, and others with whom we associate. By practicing these gospel principles, many of the social problems experienced outside the home hopefully will not be brought into it.

We could also stabilize our individual lives by having individual friends with whom we each could occasionally associate. In addition, husbands and wives together need to have friends for social interaction. "Friendship," the Prophet Joseph Smith noted, "is like Brother Turley in his blacksmith shop welding iron to iron; it unites the human family with its happy influence."[6]

A Spiritual Word of Wisdom

A spiritual Word of Wisdom would suggest that we nurture the spirit within us much the way we feed, nurture, and care for our physical bodies. How could we more fully invite into our lives the companionship of the Holy Ghost? The Lord has indicated his availability, but once again we must move . . . or change. He shows us with this analogy what we must do: "Behold, I stand at the door, and knock: if any man hear my voice, and open the door, I will come in to him." (Revelation 3:20.) He has declared, "Draw near unto me and I will draw near unto you." (D&C 88:63; see also James 4:8.) The Lord will not steer a parked car. Neither will he guide our footsteps unless we move our feet. Neither will he open a door that we keep shut against him.

Keeping the commandments is perhaps the best way to draw near to the Lord and bring his influence into our lives. (See Leviticus 26:3, 9, 11–12; John 15:10.) Each week when we partake of the sacrament, we witness that we are willing to take upon us the Lord's name, always remember him, and keep his commandments. The promise is "that [we] may always have his Spirit to be with [us.]" (D&C 20:77.) By having his Spirit more abundantly in our lives, we would be able to enjoy the "fruits" or attendant blessings of love, joy, peace, longsuffering, gentleness, goodness, and faith that the Lord has promised. (See Galatians 5:22.)

What if a husband and wife each decided to take responsibility for his or her life and change first in regards to spiritual matters? If the couple sought, as individuals as well as partners, the companionship of the Holy Ghost in their daily lives, how would they deal with the differences in their marriage? What if both husband and wife observed the patience principle, "let patience have her perfect work" (James 1:4), by exercising great patience with each other's weaknesses and shortcomings? What would happen if they withdrew their constant insistence that the other change? Would not love and harmony increase and the troublesome differences begin to disappear or be seen as less significant?

There is a fundamental truth about change in marriage. Dr. Kinder and Dr. Cowan write, "There must be a void created for any new patterns to be established. And releasing one's mate from the burden of having to meet unrealistic expectations allows him or her to perceive you in a new way and to think about being different on his or her own terms."[7]

The Prophet Joseph Smith explained the power of love and uncritical relationships: "It is a time-honored adage that love begets love. Let us pour forth love — show forth our kindness unto all mankind, and the Lord will reward us with everlasting increase; cast our bread upon the waters and we shall receive it after many days. . . . I do not dwell upon your faults, and you shall not upon mine. Charity, which is love, covereth a multitude of sins, and I have often covered up all the faults among you; but the prettiest thing is to have no faults at all. We should cultivate a meek, quiet and peaceable spirit."[8]

9

THE TEN Cs: THE FOUNDATION OF COMMITMENT, CARING, AND COMMUNICATION

There are a multitude of ways to deal with differences effectively. In my marriage classes, I focus on ten successful strategies, and to make them easy to remember, I call them the ten Cs. The next four chapters deal with these ten: commitment, caring, communication, coexistence, capitulation, compromise, collaboration, confrontation, counseling, and Christ.

All couples start to deal with their differences in marriage on the foundation of the first three Cs: commitment, caring, and communication. Think of these concepts as a triangle incorporating skills necessary to work through the differences, disagreements, conflict, and anger that arise in the marital relationship.

Commitment

COMMITMENT

The first C of dealing with differences in marriage is commitment. Every marriage begins with a statement of commitment.

Most often it is the vows that a couple make in the wedding ceremony before the officiator. Typically, the vows include words about honoring and cherishing each other for the duration of the marriage. And they often include something about staying together through difficult times. The vows in many ceremonies feature such phrases as "in sickness and in health," "for rich and for poor," and "for better or for worse." In other words, husband and wife promise not to jump ship whenever troubles arise. They will enjoy the times in their marriage when they are healthy, when they have sufficient money, and when things are going well. But they also agree to stay together when there is illness, when they don't have the money to pay their bills, and when things are not going well.

Latter-day Saints who marry in the temple not only make these worthy commitments, but also make additional covenants to be committed to righteousness as marriage partners for time (this life) and eternity (the next life). The promises of temple marriage, including the promise of being husband and wife in the hereafter, are based on keeping the commitments.

I remember one particular time in our marriage when things weren't going too well. It wasn't that Susan and I had any great problems between us, but some plans we had made didn't work out, and we were both disappointed. We had to make some major adjustments and new plans for the months ahead. After we found out the necessity to reorganize, I was sitting on a chair looking out the window. What would we do next? I wondered. Susan came over, put her arms around me, and gave me a kiss for consolation. Then she said, "We'll do whatever it takes." The significance of her statement didn't catch my attention for another few minutes, but then I realized she was recommitting. Whatever the new circumstances required, she said we would do — together. Often we think that we can succeed in contemporary marriage by just doing our best. Sometimes, though, to succeed today in marriage we just can't do our best. We must do what is necessary to succeed.

The Third Entity

When two people marry, they sometimes naïvely think that their relationship is between just two people. Little do they know or understand that the state in which they marry has a vested interest in the relationship, with guidelines and laws to which the couple must adhere if they are to legally stay married. For Christian couples, Jesus Christ also becomes a partner in the marital relationship (as does deity in most religious groups). Children's advocacy groups now claim, rightfully so, that children born in a marriage also have a moral and legal interest in the maintenance and outcome of the marriage. In addition, parents, grandparents, relatives, friends, and neighbors are affected by what a husband and wife decide to do about their marriage. So marriage is far more than a relationship between just two people.

In a marriage, a husband or wife may sometimes think "What is the best for me?" That is only natural since all of us need to watch out for our own interests in life. That may also be one of the reasons a person entered the relationship. But a healthy self-interest can slip into conceit and arrogance, which can quickly undermine a marriage. A marriage cannot succeed if two people go into it with the attitude of "What is in this for me?" or "What can I get out of this relationship?" unless the partners are equally concerned with what they are giving to the person they married. In order for contemporary marriages to survive, there must be a balance in both giving and receiving. Any extreme in either direction will cause problems. One can neither give nor receive all the time.

The scriptures indicate that love is not "puffed up" and "seeketh not her own," qualities that are the opposite of pride and selfishness. (1 Corinthians 13:4–5; Moroni 7:45.) Many times in the marriage, a husband and a wife must ask not what is best for them individually, but what is best for their marriage. And on many occasions, one or the other or both may have to yield to protect the stability and maintenance of the marital relationship.

In my marriage classes and seminars, I have often discussed what I call the third entity. I draw three circles on the chalkboard that look something like this:

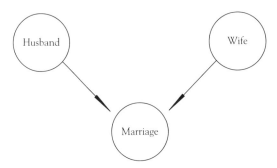

This third entity, marriage, is separate from the male and female. When we marry, we create a marital relationship that needs nurturing and protection. On occasion, situations may have to be rearranged for the benefit of the husband. Likewise, on occasion they may have to be rearranged for the benefit of the wife. But once in a while, when the marriage is frail or weakened, or otherwise needs attention, decisions must be made with the marriage in mind. It too must be protected and nourished. Commitment extends not only to each spouse, but to the third entity.

Bear and Endure All Things

The scriptures also note that love bears and endures all things. (See 1 Corinthians 13:7.) That is sometimes twisted to mean accept everything. There are some things that neither husband nor wife should have to bear or tolerate in a marriage. Physical or emotional abuse, infidelity, nonsupport, and abandonment are just a few. Love also does "not behave itself unseemly, . . . thinketh no evil; rejoiceth not in iniquity." (13:5–6.) So abusive acts and adultery are hardly compatible with love. When I read that love bears and endures all things, I think that in marriage this refers to what a couple must bear and endure together.

The thirteenth Article of Faith similarly states, "We believe all things, we hope all things, we have endured many things, and hope to be able to endure all things." Such is the commitment that a married couple must have if their marriage is to survive marriage in the turbulent and troubled times ahead. They must be committed to do whatever it takes.

CARING

The second C in dealing with differences is caring, a manifestation of love. Remember the quote from Elder B. H. Roberts in chapter seven: "In essentials let there be unity; in non-essentials, liberty; and in all things, charity!"

Sometimes we find it difficult to be caring when we are upset or angry or when we are trying to resolve a difference that has arisen. Because of the interaction and closeness that go with marriage, most of us will occasionally experience anger with our loved ones. (See chapter two.) But the goal is to try to resolve or even dissolve anger in such a way that the more desirable quality and value of caring may soon return.

Before we try to resolve a difference with our husbands or wives, we might start by asking these two questions: (1) How can I go about trying to resolve this difference with him (or her) and protect the marriage? (2) How can I try to resolve this difference in a loving and caring way? When these two questions are asked and acted upon in dealing with any difference in marriage, a framework is built upon which differences can be discussed without fear of threat, anger, or retaliation.

In marriage, the husband and wife should not only care *about* each other, but also care *for* each other. When a husband cares about his wife, what she does and thinks matters to him. When a wife cares about her husband, she places importance on how he feels and what he does. When a wife is sick, the husband cares for her, and vice versa. When the husband is well, the wife still nurtures him, builds him up, and is concerned about his welfare. The husband likewise watches over the welfare of his wife, trying to enhance her life and help her handle trials and meet challenges.

When differences arise, however, a couple sometimes forget

to be caring. Both husband and wife may need to pause and remember these words, "I care about what you say and what you feel. These things are important to me. I need to care for you, nurture you." The disagreement, the falling out, the difference that seemed so critical a few moments before suddenly is seen in a new light. Many times a couple will discover that caring will resolve a difference or make it easier to deal with.

COMMUNICATION

In each of the other four books I have written about marriage, I have included a chapter devoted to communication.[1] I have tried to write something that might be relevant for couples trying to improve their communication skills in a marital relationship. In both studying about and trying to improve my own skills in communication, I have sometimes wondered if I make it too clinical and difficult. Susan has pointed out to me that when we try to discuss matters of mutual concern, she occasionally feels she is talking to a marriage counselor and not her husband. In retrospect, she is probably right. Often I do become more concerned that we are following all the correct rules and procedures in communication than that we are trying to convey and understand the intents of our hearts. I suppose that is one of the occupational hazards of being in this field.

I heard a humorous rhyme once that I think has relevance to this topic. It goes as follows:

> A centipede was happy quite,
> Until a frog in fun
> Said, "Pray, which leg comes after which?"
> This raised her mind to such a pitch,
> She lay distracted in a ditch,
> Considering how to run.

In years past, long before all the books, tapes, and training in communication were available, many millions upon millions of husbands and wives somehow found out or learned how to talk with each other in a loving, caring way. But modern society's tendency to pyschoanalyze everything sometimes makes us like the centipede—when we sit down and try to figure out how we do things we already are doing, we sometimes become confused and freeze. This is called "analysis paralysis."

The words we choose to say, the intonation, our ability to share clear messages, our skills in listening—all are critical in communicating with a spouse. But let me share with you a few other basic skills in communication that I have learned in my own marriage and that relate to dealing with differences.

It is true that we learn by experience. (See D&C 121:39.) Many husbands and wives could, if called upon, write a book titled *How Not to Be Married!* Susan and I certainly could. Some of the most important things we learn in life are from failure. We have come to appreciate the following saying in our own marriage:

> Success comes from good judgment.
> Good judgment comes from experience.
> Experience comes from learning.
> Learning comes from failure.
> Therefore, learning from failure
>   is the key to success!

I learned early in my marriage, long before I got into marriage and family counseling, three vital concepts that have been helpful. They are *when, where,* and *why* to talk over differences of opinions, thoughts, and feelings in marriage. And I learned by trying to do it the wrong way for a long time. When these three things are taken care of, the *how* becomes much easier to figure out and accomplish.

When

We discovered soon in our marriage that we differed in our opinions and preferences on when to talk about differences, irritations, and hurt feelings. I was well aware of the biblical admonition "Let not the sun go down upon your wrath." (Ephesians 4:26.) Do it quickly, right away if possible, I thought. If something bothered me about our marriage, I wanted to talk about it and get it behind us—now! But Susan, in her usual gentle way, taught me that some times are better than others for talking things over. Trying to "never go to bed angry" was one of the worst and most futile things we ever attempted. Such a belief programs couples to talk about problems and concerns between ten to twelve P.M. This was not a good time for us (and other couples may find this to be true for them as well). Sometimes we "agreed to disagree" for a few hours and get some sleep so that we could deal with the disagreement better the next morning.

When either of us is absorbed in a project or anything that demands thought and attention, we know that this is not a good time to work through some concern. So here is what we have learned to do. One will say, "I have a concern I would like to talk over. When would be a good time?" That approach works much better than trying to insist that it be worked through immediately. I know a man who once commanded his wife "in the name of the priesthood" to sit in a chair until they resolved some difference. She sat so long she eventually passed out, and he had to help her up off the floor. That is an extreme example of prematurely and unrighteously forcing discussions before both are ready for it.

If a husband or wife, however, goes to the other spouse and indicates that there is a concern needing discussion, they can decide to arrange a time and a place where the discussion can occur. Try to arrange a time that is less hectic, when neither spouse is fatigued or hungry or distracted.

Where

Not only is the timing critical for discussions about differences, but the place of the discussion is important as well. Have you ever wondered why the Lord took people to isolated places such as mountain tops or deserts when he had something important to tell them? One reason may be that he wanted to get them away from the common routines and distractions of the day.

Sometimes you have to leave your home to have a sensitive

discussion. Get out of the house and go for a walk or a drive in the car. Perhaps you could go out to eat first and then talk over your concerns. If you think the matter is something that requires a great deal of thought and attention, maybe you can get away to a motel or some other retreat for a night or two to discuss, think, ponder, and pray. Or, if you choose to stay at home, you need to go to a room where you are alone and isolated from children, phone calls, and doorbells so that a uninterrupted discussion can occur. Some like to talk things over in the bedroom, but then the bedroom might become associated with a place where they talk through hurt feelings and concerns. One other suggestion. If possible, hold hands or put your arms around each other while you are talking. This "touch" helps keep things under control.

Why

After Susan and I got married, I soon learned the importance of talking things over, to consider why Susan and I felt or believed differently. I had my way of viewing things and Susan had hers. Both of us thought we were correct. And sometimes we became more concerned with *who* was right than *what* was right. Learning to listen to another person's point of view often brings new perspective to your own. A spouse will not only see things differently, but will often notice something the other hasn't observed.

Do you think you are always right and quite accurate in your ability to observe? Before you answer, take this three-question quiz:

Question 1: What is wrong with the following wording:

I PLEDGE ALLEGIANCE TO THE FLAG OF
OF THE UNITED STATES OF AMERICAN
AND TO THE REPUBLIC FOR WHICH IT
IT STANDS. ONE NATION, UNDER GOD,
INDIVISIBLE, WITH LIBERTY AND JUSTICE
FOR ALL.

Did you find anything wrong with the wording? Look again.
Question 2: How many Fs are there in the following sentence?

FINISHED FILES ARE THE RESULT OF YEARS OF
TOUGH SCIENTIFIC STUDY COMBINED WITH THE
ROUGH EXPERIENCE OF MANY YEARS.

How many Fs did you count? Just three? Wrong! Count again.
Question 3: *In your head* (without paper and pencil), quickly
add up the following numbers:

1000

10

1000

20

1000

30

1000

40

Just a simple adding assignment? Numerous people will answer 5000 . . . which is wrong. Try again.

Answers to the three questions:

Question 1: There are duplications of "OF" and "IT" ("TO
THE FLAG OF OF" and "TO THE REPUBLIC FOR WHICH
IT IT"). Did you find both duplications? Did you notice that
"AMERICAN" should be "AMERICA"? When things are fa-
miliar to us, we often ignore or don't pay attention to what we
think we already know.

Question 2: People report seeing anywhere from three to
eight Fs in the sentence. There are six. Most report only three
and miss the Fs in the three "OF"s because they have a V sound.
Some people also report seeing Fs in the words "ROUGH" and
"TOUGH" because the "GH" sounds like an F.

Question 3: The answer to the adding problem is 4100. Many
people give the answer as 5000 because they make the mistake
of "carrying over," moving the 1 from the hundred column to
the thousand column.

Are you always sure you're right? Can you trust only your own observations and evaluations of a situation? Will the input of others help you get a more accurate assessment of a situation?

The *when* and the *where* of dealing with differences in a marriage are as important as the content of the discussion and the skills used in communication. And when the setting is adequate, we can pay attention to new perspectives and the *why* of our spouses' thoughts and feelings, why they think and feel the way they do. Both husband and wife may lack perspective and can benefit from each other's insights.

When we pay attention to these three facets, the how of communication becomes so much easier and natural. In chapters ten to twelve, I discuss the how-to part of dealing with differences in greater detail.

10

THE TEN Cs: THE FREQUENT FOUR OF COEXISTENCE, CAPITULATION, COMPROMISE, AND COLLABORATION

In the last chapter we established a basis on which to build for dealing with our differences in marriage. That foundation includes a triangle of the first three Cs: commitment, caring, and communication. Now we are ready to proceed to the next four Cs that counselors and educators often use or suggest in helping couples work through their differences. The next four Cs are coexistence, capitulation, compromise, and collaboration.[1] Although different terms are sometimes used by various authors, the concepts are similar.

COEXISTENCE

The fourth C in dealing with differences is coexistence. The definition of *coexist* is "to live together without conflict, despite differences."[2] In contemporary language we would say to simply practice patience. We can have unity without uniformity. The first quality of love mentioned in 1 Corinthians 13:4 is long-suffering. (See also Moroni 7:45.) The patience principle is also taught in James 1:4, "Let patience have her perfect work." We simply learn to tolerate some of the behaviors or characteristics of a husband or wife. We learn to say, perhaps several times, "I can live with it."

We learned in chapter two that in marriage, our spouses most likely will not meet all our needs. The point was made that if they meet 80 percent of our needs, we should be grateful. But what do we do about the other 20 percent of our unmet needs? We try to be patient with their inability to meet them.

There is a difference between being *frustrated* and being *disappointed* in a marriage. When we are frustrated, our needs or expectations haven't been met *yet*. If we are disappointed, we believe that our needs and expectations *won't* be met. Now for a critical question. Are you frustrated with your unmet needs, or are you disappointed? How you feel about it makes quite a difference. I believe that most of us should choose to feel frustrated because we do not know what the future may yet hold. If we learn to talk through our differences and learn to work on our unmet needs, perhaps our spouses will be more willing to try to meet them. But before we try to change our marriage partners to meet our needs, we first should focus on what we need to do or correct to make more loving, caring, and better spouses of ourselves (the change-first principle).

Not long ago one of my students at BYU came to talk to me about her roommate who was engaged to be married in just a few months. The student said her engaged roommate was untidy, and she felt compelled to inform the future husband. I was intrigued that a roommate would feel such a compulsion and asked a few more questions. In her answers, I sensed some jealousy that my student was not engaged and her roommate was. I suggested this, and my student hesitantly admitted to some jealousy.

Then I inquired about the untidiness of the roommate. My student went into a long elaboration to document her claims. The more she talked, however, the more I felt the problem to be with my student and not with her roommate. My student had a narrow tolerance level and simply wasn't very patient. She said her engaged roommate occasionally left clothes on the floor. And once in a while she wouldn't put all her dirty dishes in the sink. Once during the semester she had failed to clean the bathroom when it was her turn. That was about the extent of her untidiness.

Should the roommate inform the engaged fellow of the untidiness of his new fiancee? Absolutely not! Let him find out for himself, if indeed she really was messy. In such a problem, if it was a problem, being patient and tolerant would help. The husband could simply learn to coexist with her clothes, dishes, and bathroom sink unless the untidiness became excessive for him.

What is on your list from the exercise for identifying your differences (chapter seven) that you can learn to tolerate? Where can you be more patient? What can you learn to live with? Many if not most of the nonessentials could fit into this category. And by learning to become more tolerant and patient, you too can learn to say, "I can live with this." I can coexist.

CAPITULATION

The fifth C in learning to deal with differences in marriage is capitulation, or simply giving in. Many times you will find that, for the sake of the marriage, you can let your spouse have or do something his or her way. There are at least two times when you may want to capitulate, or give in, to your spouse. The first is when you are wrong and later find out and admit it. When Susan and I sometimes differ on an issue, she is usually right. (Not all the time, but most of the time.) She has a keen sense of what would be best for us to do in our marriage and for our family. When I later find out that she is right, and it usually doesn't take very long, I have to go back and apologize, then do whatever it was her way. On a similar note President Spencer W. Kimball admonished:

> Many young people labor and live under false notions, feeling that a marriage contract, and especially if it is a temple marriage, solves all the problems; and many people further think that marriage is a sort of perpetual motion program. Once set in motion by a marriage ceremony, it will never run down. I want to tell you that there are no marriages that can ever be happy ones unless two people work at it.
>
> When problems affect a couple the easy thing is to stand

on one's pride and quarrel, yielding not an inch, and to permit those differences to continue to get bigger and more cankerous until each party seeks comfort from friends, relatives, and finally a dissolution of the marriage. The hard thing, when problems arise, is to swallow pride, eat humble pie, analyze the situation, accept the blame that is properly due . . . and develop the courage to say, "I'm sorry."[3]

The second time you may consider capitulation is when neither opinion is necessarily "right" or "wrong." For instance, what if a husband and wife disagree on which movie to see on a particular evening? Or, what about deciding on the best time to clean the living-room drapes? Should our thirteen-year-old daughter have a sleep-over at our house tonight or go to her friend's house for a sleep-over? Some differences in marriage do not necessarily have right or wrong preferences. They are simply opinions or options, either of which may have some merit or value. How do you know when to capitulate or give in on such occasions?

The Scale of One to Ten

One good indicator of when to use the fifth C is to use an imaginary scale. How do you use such a scale in marriage? You simply ask your spouse, "On a scale of one to ten, how committed are you to doing it your way?"

For example, Bob wants to go to his parents' home for Thanksgiving this year, whereas RaNae wants to go to hers. The families live several hundred miles apart, so Bob and RaNae can visit only one set of parents for the holiday. They therefore use the scale of one to ten to measure their levels of commitment to their preferences. RaNae states that on the scale, she is nine. She has sensed in recent telephone conversations with her mother that her mother is not physically well. RaNae would like to visit her parents not only for Thanksgiving, but also to see how her mother is doing in regard to her health.

Bob states that his preference on the scale is about a six. His nephew, whom he has not seen for three years, has just returned from a mission, and Bob was looking forward to seeing him. After the 9/6 comparison, Bob realizes that going to see RaNae's parents for Thanksgiving is very important to Ranae. He still retains his desire for his preference, but seeing that RaNae is more committed to her preference than he is to his, Bob wisely yields, or capitulates, and they make plans to visit RaNae's parents for the holiday.

As this case demonstrates, husbands and wives sometimes have not only different opinions or preferences, but also varying levels of commitment to their choices. Using the scale can help ascertain those levels of commitment so individuals may know when it is best to acquiesce or capitulate in a marriage.

Capitulation, Not Martyrdom

Before we leave the fifth C of capitulation, however, let me give just a few words of caution. If you are going to yield or give in, don't become a martyr in the process. Most of us can recall some incident in our lives when a brother, sister, friend, or parent finally gave in but made everyone miserable in the process. I'm embarrassed to say that Susan and I have done this. A few years ago when our son Brian was a junior in high school, he wanted to have a party one Saturday night in our basement for a large number of people. Susan and I didn't want to have it because of the late notice, the number of people involved, and the extra effort involved in housecleaning on an already hectic weekend. We talked the matter over together with Brian for a few days and finally "gave in." (We capitulated.)

Partly in jest, but partly not, I kept reminding Brian that week as we made preparations, of the inconvenience the party was creating. I was playing the martyr role. But unknown to me, Susan was doing the same. She was less than enthusiastic in planning the food for his guests (just how much pizza can fourteen teenagers eat?) and soliciting the cooperation of our other children to help clean "for Brian's party." Finally Brian came to us and said he was going to call the party off. Even though he appreciated our willingness to let him have his friends visit, he said it was not worth all the hassle we were putting him through. Later than night Susan and I talked the situation over with the family and realized that Brian was right. Even though we had given in to his request, we had become "martyrs" for the cause. Such a tendency should be avoided in the capitulation process.

A marriage also suffers if either the husband or the wife does all or most of the capitulating. Both must be willing to give or yield for the sake of the marriage, the third entity. However, when one capitulates to the other all or most of the time, the relationship becomes unbalanced and turns into what counselors call a master/slave, or dominant/submissive, relationship. Slaves give in to their masters.

Sometimes a spouse will capitulate for an equally unhealthy reason: he or she doesn't want the responsibility of making the decision or being responsible for its consequences. When one spouse continuously says to the other, "You decide," it could be as much an act of irresponsibility as a signal of cooperation. And the one having to make all or most of the decisions often tires of this arrangement. Husbands and wives not only need to share the responsibility for making decisions, but also need to be willing to take the responsibility for the choices once they are made.

COMPROMISE

When we use the sixth C in dealing with differences, we learn to compromise — negotiate or bargain. The dictionary definition of compromise is "a settlement in which each side makes concessions; something midway."[4] When we compromise, we usually yield to a common ground of interest or agreement. Neither spouse gets all of what they want, but both will usually get some of what they want.

Suppose a couple agrees to go on a vacation. The husband wants to go one place, the wife, another. On the scale of one to ten, they both are at an eight — both are rather committed to their individual preferences, and the commitment is about equal. They could (1) coexist and not go anywhere; one could (2) capitulate and go where the other wants to go; or they could (3) compromise by selecting a third vacation spot of mutual attraction.

I firmly believe that almost all differences, particularly the nonessential ones, can be solved by compromise through negotiation, thereby either removing them or lessening their intensity. This is true with perhaps 90 percent or more of the differences a couple may list in the exercise for identifying differences (chapter seven). We can learn to compromise by negotiation or bargaining.

Some husbands and wives appear offended when I talk about bargaining in marriage. But if we look at the past, we will realize that we have, perhaps unknowingly, already been bargaining with our spouses. When we say things like "If you'll do this, I'll do that," we are bargaining. We work a deal when we negotiate such things as "I'll take the car to be serviced if you'll clean up the kitchen"; "If you'll write down your checks in the register, I will enter them on the computer to keep track of our finances"; "If you'll go with me to the football game, I'll go with you to the symphony." All these are typical illustrations of negotiating or bargaining for a compromise.

On occasion some couples may negotiate in a moment of irritation by making a demand: "If you don't do such and such, then I will (or won't) do such and such." If used with discretion, it is still another way a couple may negotiate or compromise. "If you don't put your dirty socks in the hamper, I will not wash them" can be an effective and reasonable use of the demand.

A couple tried this technique several years ago. I was training to be a marriage counselor at Florida State University, and a few of us were undergoing some of the training at a community center. A young wife about three years into her marriage came to see me one day. She loved her husband and had no intention of leaving or divorcing him. He had simply been raised by a mother who catered to his every whim, which included picking up his dirty clothes, washing and folding them, and then neatly putting them back in his room. Unfortunately he carried this expectation into his marriage. He wanted his wife to do the same. She said she was willing to wash the clothes and even fold them, but she was not willing to pick up after him as his mother had done all those years.

After talking the matter over with me, she thought she would try negotiation. She decided, and her husband later agreed, that she would only wash the dirty clothes that were put in the clothes hamper. He was rather good-natured about the matter, realizing that his mother had spoiled him in regard to clean clothes. Both agreed to the compromise. If the dirty clothes, mostly socks and underwear, were left lying on the floor, she wouldn't wash them. After a few weeks, the compromise began to work. With a little playful bargaining, this couple worked through a difference that had become a source of irritation for her. Left unattended, it could easily have led to conflict and anger. Could it have led to divorce? Who knows?

COLLABORATION

When we learn to collaborate, the seventh C of dealing with differences in marriage, we are learning, as the dictionary defines it, "to work with someone."[5] This C requires the most mature behavior of the frequent four, coexistence, capitulation, compromise, and collaboration. Collaboration takes more effort than the other three, but it is a skill I believe most married couples should try to develop.

When we coexist, capitulate, or compromise, some of our needs are not met. When we coexist, we just live with the difference and do nothing. Sometimes this is necessary in marriage, but it still doesn't alleviate the irritation or concern we initially feel. When we capitulate, we acknowledge that the other person has a greater need, interest in, or stronger commitment to his or her preference. In a stable marriage, both husband and wife should be willing to yield or give in on occasion. When we compromise, both will have some of their needs met, but neither will have all of their needs met. So in all three instances, there is sort of a win/lose situation.

With the seventh C of collaboration, however, we create a

win-win relationship.[6] The husband and wife work together until ultimately both their goals or needs are met. The husband's needs become the wife's needs, the wife's needs become the husband's needs, and they both work together until both needs are attained.

Suppose, for instance, that a young couple in college become engaged. They will have limited financial resources, but both desire to graduate with a four-year college degree. They also agree that both of their degrees are important. But can they continue attending school at the same time? After a long discussion, they decide that because of their financial straits, only one will be able to continue his or her education. Traditionally, the wife is the one who drops out of school to support her husband. Suppose in this situation both he and she are equally intent on her graduating. The only question is "when." On the scale of one to ten, both are tens on how they feel about school. Believing he will be the major bread winner in the future, he and his parents think he should graduate first. She disagrees. What should they do?

They could just coexist, say nothing, and live with the difference and circumstances as they exist and see what happens. She could capitulate and yield to his education at the sacrifice of her own. Or, they could compromise, the husband going one semester while the wife works and then reversing the situation the following semester. Or they could both go part-time to school, which would take longer, but both would eventually graduate.

But what if they collaborate? What if they look at the problem differently, trying to find ways both could continue their educations and graduate on schedule? What would they do? Her graduation would still be as important to him as his own. The same would be true of her feelings toward his graduation. Rather than perceiving college graduation as a problem dividing them, they would try to figure out ways both might continue. Perhaps they could apply for scholarships, grants for financial aid, or student loans heretofore not considered. Would or could their parents help financially so she could graduate? Maybe they would both go to school full-time during the fall and winter semesters and then both work somewhere for the summer to earn enough money for the following year. Note that the process in collaboration is equally as important as the outcome. To make this a win/win situation, how can both work together to accomplish their individual and collective goals?

Another couple discovered that they made one thousand dollars more than expected after completing a project they both had worked on. She wanted to buy a grandfather clock for their hallway. He wanted to buy a rather expensive hunting rifle and some extra camping equipment. What should they do? Settle for a little chimer and a pistol? No. They both realized how much the other wanted the items (tens on the scale), so they worked together to get both the grandfather clock and the rifle. They sold some of the things they didn't need, and both worked at another project to raise the extra money. In the end, she had her grandfather clock, and he had his rifle.

When we lay the foundation of commitment, communication, and caring, we find that collaboration is much easier to do. We have learned our spouses' wants and needs, and we can work together to attain them.

PLANNING A WEDDING AND
DEALING WITH DIFFERENCES

A great need arises for using the first seven Cs in planning a wedding. Planning a wedding is usually the first major project that an engaged couple have to undertake together. And not surprisingly, differences arise. During the planning phase of the wedding ceremony and reception, a couple experience a great need to use all of the first seven Cs: commitment, caring, communication, coexistence, capitulation, compromise, and collaboration.

I observed this process firsthand during the months when I was writing this book. My daughter Tammy returned from the Ohio Cleveland Mission in October 1991. In December she became engaged to a fine young man, Darrell Bevell from Scottsdale, Arizona, who had also served in the same mission. They set their wedding date for June 5, 1992, which was not only

Susan's and my wedding anniversary, but also that of Darrell's parents, Jim and Donna Bevell. The plans went forward and everyone was happy. Then a problem arose.

Darrell had been a successful quarterback on the football team at Chaparral High School in Scottsdale, where his father, Jim, was the football coach. Darrell had attended Northern Arizona University for one year before going on his mission. After completing his mission, he was recruited by the University of Wisconsin in Madison to play football. To make a long and complex story simple and short, the coaches encouraged Darrell and Tammy to wait until his first football season was over before they married. (And in hindsight, I must admit they were right. Their concerns for Darrell and Tammy were genuine.)

To say the least, differences of opinion arose. Should they go ahead with their marriage plans on June 5 or wait until December 1992, after the football season was over? After many long discussions they finally decided to postpone their wedding for six months until December. Darrell enrolled that spring at the University of Wisconsin, worked out during the summer, and attended the fall football camp. Tammy stayed home with us and worked full-time to save some money. There was no question that they were in love, cared about each other, and were committed to their marriage. And believe me, they communicated often and for long periods of time . . . by phone! She flew to Wisconsin several times during the six months to see Darrell play as the starting quarterback (and to talk to the coaches)! Both she and Darrell had to exercise patience and coexist with the situation imposed upon them.

During this time, I noted that Tammy and Darrell used almost all the first seven Cs in reconsidering their wedding plans. They were committed to each other, cared about each other, and communicated at least once a day by phone. They did not use words like coexist, capitulate, compromise, and collaborate. (They hadn't yet read the draft of this book.) But I did notice that they exercised great patience with each other. They knew when to give in on items where they differed, yielding when necessary. On some issues where they differed, on the one-to-ten scale, they were both at ten. (Sometimes to me it sounded as if they were both at eleven!) They had to negotiate and even bargain over some differences that arose. (The phone bills testify of that!)

Most important, they agreed to work together to do what was necessary to marry in the Salt Lake Temple December 22, 1992, which they did. As newlyweds, Darrell and Tammy Bevell returned to the University of Wisconsin in Madison, where they looked forward to the upcoming football season when Darrell would once again play quarterback for the Wisconsin Badgers.

I pay tribute to two young people who somehow were able to work through some very difficult circumstances, with enormous differences of opinions at times, so that they could marry each other. They have, early in their relationship, learned to deal with some of their differences. And all I can say, as father of the bride, may they continue to do so.

11

THE TEN Cs: THE SPECIAL CIRCUMSTANCES OF CONFRONTATION AND COUNSELING

When married couples approach their differences by laying the foundation of commitment, caring, and communication, they can deal with the majority of their differences by using the four Cs of coexistence, capitulation, compromise, and collaboration. In some marriages, however, a few situations may arise where these strategies will not suffice. There may be times when confrontation or counseling will be necessary.

CONFRONTATION

The word *confront* means "to face boldly" or "to bring face to face."[1] Occasionally in marriage, one spouse may confront another over a matter causing some concern. A partner may be late for church or forget an important engagement that the couple had planned to attend, and the other will become irritated or angry. The husband or wife then confronts the other, even though these mishaps are day-to-day matters that really do not jeopardize the marriage. Most of these day-to-day occurrences are usually better resolved using one or more of the seven Cs discussed thus far. The eighth C of confrontation should actually be reserved for differences or issues of great importance that absolutely must be resolved if the marriage is to continue.

Every marital relationship has what are called core symbols—circumstances, behaviors, or attitudes needed to get married and stay married. They are issues significant enough that they could lead one to choose not to marry someone. Or, if the issues arise after the wedding, they might lead a person to divorce the other if the concerns were not resolved.

What are some examples of core symbols? Most would list fidelity or sexual responsibility, honesty, and some degree of personal hygiene. Included in the list are dangerous or debilitating behaviors that could escalate into even worse problems. Suppose, for instance, a husband or wife is frequently "seeing" a member of the opposite sex. Maybe he or she has an addiction to alcohol, drugs, or gambling. What if a spouse did something illegal or repeatedly broke some law? Perhaps a spouse intentionally cheated on his or her income tax report each year and you know about it. What if the husband or wife is a Latter-day Saint and lies to the bishop or stake president on a matter of importance?

All these situations directly involve you as a married person and, to a lesser degree, your children if you have them. What do you do when you differ over some of these more important issues in marriage? Many of these fall into the category of essential differences.

What if, for example, your husband is repeatedly doing something illegal, say poaching deer or some other kind of wildlife? He does it, he says, because the family needs the food. You know it is illegal, and you do not want him to continue the illegal practice. What do you do?

Perhaps your wife works in a large corporation and spends a great deal of time with a certain man. They travel to other cities with other employees from the company and stay overnight "for business purposes." You sense that the amount of time they spend together is increasing. What do you do?

Maybe your husband wants to excel in his profession and spends sixty to seventy hours a week at work. Even when he's home, he has little contact with you or the children, thinking about his work or other obligations. You start to feel resentful and alienated from him. What should you do?

Or what if your wife has started drinking excessive amounts of alcohol. It started out as social drinking but has now become a problem not only for her, but for the rest of the family as well. What do you do?

In all these extreme cases, one need not necessarily coexist (learn to live with it), capitulate (give in to the dubious life-style), compromise (negotiate for better conditions), or collab-orate (work together to accomplish differing goals). Obviously some things will have to change if the marriage is to continue. This is where the husband or wife "faces boldly" and brings the issue "face to face." (May I point out again for emphasis that confrontation is used infrequently in most marriages. It should be reserved for those differences that, if left unattended, could lead to divorce.) So how does one "face boldly" and bring the issue "face to face" with an erring spouse?

A Book "Thief"

A few years ago, in a lecture at BYU Education Week, I mentioned the topic of marriage partners who felt they were losing a spouse to some kind of addiction, to another person, to work, or to anything else causing estrangement. I held up the book *Love Must Be Tough: New Hope for Families in Crisis* by Dr. James Dobson. I told them that this book, written by a well-known Christian counselor, was written specifically for such people. In the first chapter Dr. Dobson warns such couples of the well-meaning but questionable advice they get from friends and even some counselors during this time of crisis in their marriage. He notes:

> The book you are about to read provides an alternative [to immediate divorce] for those in the midst of family crises. My purpose in writing it has been to offer some practical tools — some understandings — which should be useful in drawing an apathetic husband or wife back in the direction of commitment. It may be surprising to learn that human

conflict, *if properly managed,* can be the vehicle for trans-forming an unstable relationship into a vibrant, healthy marriage. On the other hand, the wrong response in mo-ments of crisis can quickly smother the dying embers of love.[2]

After reading this statement to the group, I related a few of Dobson's suggestions. When the lecture ended, a woman in her thirties came up to the front, took Dr. Dobson's book off the podium, and said, "Brother Barlow, I'll bring your book back tomorrow." Before I could say anything or stop her, she left with my book under her arm. Let me mention that I hesitate to loan out books because they often are not returned. (Borrowing with-out returning is just a subtle form of theft.) But in this situation I had no chance to say no.

The next morning, however, she was good to her word and brought my book back. After my lecture that day, she stayed after and told me an interesting story. Her husband was a busy LDS physician, devoting enormous hours to his profession at the expense of her and their children. In addition, he had acknowl-edged that he was "seeing" one of the single nurses with whom he worked at the hospital. The wife was devastated when he admitted that he was spending time with another woman. The woman who "borrowed" my book for one day said she came to BYU Education Week praying to know what she should do in her marriage.

She loved her husband and wanted to stay with him on two conditions: (1) he quit seeing the nurse, and (2) he devote more time to her and their children. She had stayed up almost all night reading *Love Must Be Tough* in the BYU dormitory where she was staying during the week. At an early hour in the morning she came to the conclusion that she had her answer. She thanked me for introducing Dr. Dobson's book to her.

How to Confront

What were some of the strategies she read in his book that night? First, this book is unusual in that you *do not* have your spouse read it with you.[3] It is a strategy for the spouse who is seriously contemplating ending the marriage and must do the confronting. Briefly, here is the process he recommends:

1. *Recommit and clarify:* Before you confront a spouse on a certain matter, you recommit to the marriage relationship. Tell the person why you married him or her and, if possible, declare the love that exists.

2. *Confront:* This is where the eighth C is appropriate. Building on your statement of recommitment, you communicate as clearly as possible your concern about the behavior or action that is causing you pain (seeing another person, for example). *The confrontation comes when you declare you will no longer stay in the relationship if such behavior continues!* But the choice is for the erring spouse to make.

3. *Open the door:* In confrontation, you indicate to the spouse that he or she is free to leave the marriage if the inappropriate behavior does not change. Dobson gives this saying: "If you love something, set it free. If it comes back to you, it's yours. If it doesn't come back, it never was yours in the first place."[4]

Some husbands and wives may be alarmed at the suggestion of allowing a spouse to leave. It may be risky because the spouse may actually choose to leave. But the reality is that the concerned spouse likely was in the process of losing him or her anyway if the undesirable behavior continued. Giving a spouse permission to leave the marriage is indeed risky, but it is far less risky than allowing the questionable behavior to continue.

Quite a few husbands or wives who are doing erratic things in a marriage are looking for a way out of marriage. Once they are given the opportunity to leave, they face a new question: "Am I really going to leave my marriage and family?" Faced with the reality, the spouse must fully consider the consequences of his or her actions. In many situations, the spouse reconsiders the options and chooses to stay. If the situation is left unchallenged, it will deteriorate, and the end of the marriage is only a matter of time. So giving a spouse the option to leave may be a good strategy if, indeed, the spouse is already on the way out.

There is a scripture in 1 Corinthians 7:12–15 that seems to substantiate Dr. Dobson's strategy. Paul's admonition is written to those Saints in Corinth who were married to nonbelievers. The advice, however, is an "open the door" strategy, relevant to the kinds of situations we've been discussing: "If any brother hath a wife that believeth not, and she be pleased to dwell with him, let him not put her away [divorce her]. And the woman which hath an husband that believeth not, and if he be pleased to dwell with her, let her not leave him. For the unbelieving husband is sanctified by the wife, and the unbelieving wife is sanctified by the husband: else were your children unclean; but now they are holy. *But if the unbelieving depart, let him [or her] depart.* A brother or a sister is not under bondage [or bound] in such cases." (Italics added.)

In applying the eighth C of confrontation, you need to consider the time frame for change. A husband or wife may request that some undesirable behavior in a spouse stop immediately. Such situations might include seeing or "dating" a member of the opposite sex while married or pursuing something illegal. I have counseled many LDS members whose husbands or wives are in such a situation. One does not use the frequent four in such situations. A husband or wife should not coexist, capitulate, compromise, or collaborate with a spouse who wants to date another person! That is ludicrous! When we marry, we agree to forsake all others, or as modern-day revelation indicates, we "cleave unto" or be with a spouse "*and none else*"! (D&C 42:22.)

Neither should we just live with, give in to, or negotiate with a spouse who wants to do unethical or unlawful acts. Can you imagine the conversation? "Honey, just sign these illegal documents for income tax rebates just two more years and then we'll stop cheating." Some things in a marriage have to stop *immediately* if the marriage is going to survive.

There may be other instances, however, when one spouse confronts another, and a little more patience may have to be exercised. If a husband or wife becomes addicted to alcohol or some other drug, for instance, he or she probably cannot withdraw immediately. If a marriage partner agrees to seek professional help, however, or enter some kind of rehabilitation program, that might be sufficient for the other spouse to stay in the marriage a while longer. There may be some other instances where the desired changes may take some time to make. A husband or wife involved in such a marriage would then set some kind of reasonable time frame for this to occur. In these special circumstances, outside help might be required.

COUNSELING

We now come to the ninth C of dealing with differences in marriage, counseling, which means "to give advice or recommend a plan."[5] When a husband and wife develop serious problems over the differences they experience in their marriage, they often seek advice from others. Sometimes such advice is given unsolicited. Friends, people at work, peers, relatives, family members, horoscopes, palm readers, newspaper columnists (and I have been one), books (like this one), tapes, and seminars may all give suggestions. Some of the advice is good and helpful. Other advice is questionable and often expensive. And some of it is downright dangerous because we receive it at a time when we are most vulnerable. This is particularly so if it comes from someone we trust or we feel cares about us. We might do what they say regardless of what they suggest.

During the past few years, we have seen the rise on late-night television of 1–900 numbers for psychics who, for about $5 a minute, will give you "personal attention" and advice and will promise to solve your problems in a twenty-minute phone call. (If you figure out the cost of such "counseling" services, you come up with a figure of about $240 to $300 an hour, three or four times the current consultation fee for professional counseling.) This says something about the desperate condition many people seeking consultation are in.

Where should Latter-day Saints go for consultation and counseling? Interestingly enough, we should start with our spouses. We often will turn to everyone else but a husband or wife when we have marital problems. Scriptures, both ancient and modern, declare that we should seek them out first. One example states: "If thy brother or sister [or spouse] offend thee, thou shalt take him or her between him or her and thee *alone*; and if he or she confess thou shalt be reconciled." (D&C 42:88; italics added. See also section on reconciliation in chapter twelve, pages 123–24.)

There is a tendency to turn to peers or friends for advice when we have serious marital problems. While the trend is understandable, it is a questionable practice. Friends are seldom unbiased and may even take sides. A natural impulse, as noted in chapter three, is to seek verification of our own, sometimes distorted views of the marital situation. Another reason I would hesitate to seek advice from friends is that they seldom keep confidences, even when they intend to keep quiet. Private information often becomes public knowledge by the indiscretions of friends in whom we confide. Gossiping is not the only way people can be indiscreet. I cannot tell you how many friendships I know have been ruined because someone confided something to another and the confidence was not kept.

Still another reason not to go to friends with marital problems is the kind of advice they might give you. This is particularly critical if the advice giver is having problems in his or her own marriage. In this case, it is the nearly blind leading those with blurred vision, and they are both still quite likely to fall into the ditch. (See Matthew 15:14.) You'll need friends long after your marital concerns are over. Sharing personal confidences about marital concerns changes friendships. And once the marriage crisis is past, the friendship will never be the same because they "know" what went on. Reserve your friends for just that . . . friends. You'll need friends in addition to a marriage partner while being married, so don't burden the friendship with details of your situation.

How about family members? Should we take our problems and concerns to them? The same general advice about friends applies to family. They seldom remain unbiased, they often take sides, and we'll need to relate with family members after our crises are over. And quite simply, family members are so close to the situation that they sometimes give either bad advice or advice that favors one or the other. And family members have also been known not to keep confidences or secrets.

If we should be hesitant to consult with friends, family members, "Psychic Sally," the horoscope in the newspaper, or the local palm reader about our marital concerns, to whom should we go?

After going to their spouses, Latter-day Saints, I believe, should counsel with their bishops. I would hesitate to share personal or intimate matters about my marriage with home and visiting teachers for the same reasons noted about family and friends. Home and visiting teachers can provide support and love, but the discussion of the actual problems falls within the bishop's stewardship. Bishops are called to direct the temporal and spiritual affairs in their wards. By the nature of his calling, a bishop has the right to divine guidance in dealing with married couples in his ward. Latter-day Saints would do well to seek such help first. In addition, as with other areas of personal concern, bishops know the importance of keeping matters confidential.

The reason for this confidentiality is noted in the Doctrine and Covenants: "If any shall offend in secret, he or she shall be rebuked in secret, that he or she may have opportunity to confess in secret to him or her whom he or she has offended, and to God, *that the church may not speak reproachfully of him or her.*" (42:92; italics added.)

LDS Social Services

The LDS Church provides marital and family counseling for its members through LDS Social Services, which is available in most areas where Church members are located. Latter-day Saints professionally trained in counseling provide the services offered through this resource.

When the marital concerns become too complicated and complex, bishops may also refer some LDS couples to competent professionals in the community who are not affiliated with LDS Social Services but who agree to counsel within LDS values and guidelines. The counselors may or may not be Church members. They have, however, usually proven themselves in previous counseling sessions with Latter-day Saints and have gained the confidence of local bishops and stake presidents.

Do Latter-day Saint couples sometimes need skilled professional help? The answer is yes, and Church leaders are aware of the need. At a meeting of AMCAP, the Association of Mormon Counselors and Psychotherapists, one general authority gave this analogy. He said he had a large grandfather clock that was a priceless family heirloom. It worked for many years, much to the delight of the family. Then one day it broke down. This particular clock had a rather complicated mechanism that drove it. The general authority said that the clock needed to be fixed, but he wouldn't trust it to an ordinary repairman. He wanted someone who had the skills and training necessary to fix his valued grandfather clock. Some LDS marriages in trouble are like that, he said. They are more complicated than others, and sometimes they need the more skilled help of professionals who are trained and who possess the specialized skills.

The vast majority of bishops offer invaluable service to couples who need assistance in dealing with differences in their marriages. But on occasion, some marriages, like the grandfather clock, may require additional or more skilled help.

Professional Counseling

Either under the direction of their local bishop or stake president, through LDS Social Services, or on their own, some Latter-day Saint couples may want to solicit the help of a professional marriage counselor in the community. Let me give just a few suggestions if this is the case.

First, seek referrals through Church leaders for such counseling. There are many people who call themselves counselors. Most of them have something to offer, but some don't. Running an ad in the paper or putting a sign in the window advertising "counseling services" does not qualify a person to help others. You don't want to take your grandfather clock to a novice or someone who just switched to clock fixer because he or she likes to "fix things." Some states have licensing laws for counselors, so that is something you can check. If you live in a state that does not require licensing, you can still check if the counselor belongs to a professional organization that offers certification indicating a certain level of professional competence. Two such organizations are the American Association for Marriage and Family Counseling (AAMFT) and the American Psychological Association (APA). If a religious leader does not have a referral for you, your physician may be able to recommend a counselor.

Second, you should learn something about the counselor's training as well. This information is often provided in a pamphlet or brochure or can be obtained from a receptionist in the office. Some professionals specialize in particular techniques, so you may want to ask about their specialties. (As an analogy, would you go to an anesthesiologist to receive treatment for lower back problems?) Remember, the counselor is working for you and not the reverse. During the first session, share your immediate concerns with the counselor and ask if he or she can help you with your differences. And *insist* at some point in the therapy that the counselor see you and your spouse together. I get nervous when I hear of frequent sessions involving only one spouse even though the original concern involves both marriage partners. Let the counselor know if he or she is actually helping you with the problem or problems you had when you entered counseling.

Third, check costs and ability to pay before you actually begin. Counseling is an expensive experience but one well worth the expense if the goals of the consultation are identified at the beginning and eventually attained. And in fairness to the counselors, working through problems takes time. Before you seek counseling, check with your health insurance carrier. Most will not pay for marriage counseling. Some insurance companies pay a portion, such as 20, 40, or 50 percent. Interestingly enough, most health carriers will pay for private consultation but not

marriage counseling. However, many health maintenance organizations (HMOs) do include marriage counseling services.

You will also need to know the fee per visit. In 1993, fees
ranged anywhere from fifty to one hundred dollars per session
depending on the length of the session (usually forty-five minutes)
and the level of training the counselor has attained. Some couples
run up counseling bills of over one thousand dollars only to find
that their health care provider does not cover marriage counseling. Such a situation could lead to law suits and small claim
courts, which can undo much of the good that the counseling
accomplished.

If couples prepare, seek adequate referrals, go into counseling
with a positive attitude, work with the counselor they have
chosen, and follow the counseling or guidelines they receive, the
majority will likely experience beneficial results. Just acknowl-
edging the problem, going to a counselor, and talking the situation over in a private setting are often helpful steps to most
couples.

Let me add, however, a few notes of caution. No counselor
has a magic bag of tricks. See him or her as your coach or guide.
Most of the significant things that happen during counseling don't
happen in the office but in the home. Six to ten hours with any
counselor will not always produce long-term changes. But with
the help of a counselor's objective insights, skills, and suggestions,
many couples do learn to deal with differences that have become
increasingly difficult to manage.

Seek professional consultation when appropriate and when
needed. Don't let your problems become so intense or immense
that nothing can be done. Couples who have waited too long
for help turn marriage counseling into little more than combat
surgery. The damage has been so prolonged and intense that little
can be done about the situation except to stop the bleeding and
begin to aid in the healing process. Nevertheless, in time, even
the most severe marital cases can usually be helped by skilled,
professional assistance.

12

THE TEN Cs: THE TREMENDOUS POWER OF CHRIST

Professional consultation is sometimes called *horizontal* help. We look outward to other people who might appropriately assist us with our concerns. But as Latter-day Saints, we have another source of help.

Where else can we go when we need help? We could seek *vertical* help, looking not out but up! There is an abundance of divine guidance offered by Jesus Christ to his disciples. Note also that Jesus was called "Counsellor" by Isaiah. (9:6.) Seeking spiritual guidance in our lives is so important that I felt I should devote an entire chapter to the topic.

As an introduction, let me cite a scriptural passage from the Old Testament, New Testament, Doctrine and Covenants, and the Book of Mormon:

"Trust in the Lord with all thine heart; and lean not unto thine own understanding. In all thy ways acknowledge him, and he shall direct thy paths." (Proverbs 3:5–6.)

"If any of you lack wisdom, let him ask of God, that giveth to all men liberally, and upbraideth not; and it shall be given him. But let him ask in faith, nothing wavering. For he that wavereth is like a wave of the sea driven with the wind and tossed." (James 1:5–6.)

"Be thou humble; and the Lord thy God shall lead thee by the hand, and give thee answer to thy prayers." (D&C 112:10.)

"Feast upon the words of Christ; for behold, *the words of*

Christ will tell you all things what ye should do." (2 Nephi 32:3; italics added.)

Latter-day Saint couples should be grateful that divine assistance is available to help them with their marital and family concerns. I am absolutely convinced that Jesus Christ and his teachings have guidelines and principles to help his disciples deal with differences in marriage. This belief comes not only from experiences in my own marriage, but also from experiences that other Latter-day Saints have shared with me.

THE YOUNG EXECUTIVE

One day after speaking at Education Week at BYU, a young couple asked if they could talk to me for a few minutes. During my speech I had mentioned that we need to pay more attention to gospel principles to help us in our marriage and family relations rather than rely totally on counselors and therapists. When difficulties arise, we need to go for vertical help as well as horizonal help.

During the few minutes we spent together, the husband related a very interesting episode he and his wife had encountered in their marriage. He was a Latter-day Saint in his early thirties and a successful executive in a prominent business in his home town. His success had led him to ignore his wife and new baby daughter. He said he worked sixty to seventy hours a week at the office and often took work home to complete. His job required him to travel a great deal, and he was gone from home many times on weekends. This meant he not only was spending inadequate amounts of time with his wife and daughter, but also was missing Sunday church services.

At first he tried to attend church at wards in the cities where he had to conduct business, but after a time he stopped making the effort. He became involved with a woman colleague at his office, spending a great deal of time with her. At first the relationship was supposedly businesslike and professional, but then they became emotionally attached to each other. A sexual encounter loomed as a likely possibility. Then, about the time he was promoted to the high-salaried position he was aspiring to, his wife filed for divorce.

The young executive said he made several attempts at reconciliation. He reluctantly agreed to see their bishop, who suggested that they needed professional counseling. That avenue was pursued but to no avail — the damage had apparently been done. They finally entered the waiting period before their divorce would be final.

The husband became a little tearful as he continued his story. He realized that he would lose his young wife by divorce and that subsequently his relationship with his little daughter would be limited. The divorce and final separation seemed inevitable.

So he made a decision. As a priesthood holder and returned missionary, he still wanted to retain his membership in the Church and reestablish his relationship with the Savior. In essence, he decided not so much to "come unto Christ" as to "return to Christ." During the few weeks before the finalization of the divorce, he began praying alone and fasting periodically. He stopped seeing and traveling with the woman at his office. He attended his priesthood and other Church meetings regularly for the first time in several months. He started to study the gospel and to get more involved in Church service. He examined his heart and tried to bring spirituality into his life. He did all these things fully expecting that his wife and child would soon leave him. But unknown to him, his wife was observing him. (As he was telling me about this episode in their lives, she was holding on to his arm, also in tears.)

The wife then continued the story. She said she noted some sincere and genuine changes in him as he tried drawing closer to the Lord. When the time came for her to sign the final divorce papers, she called her attorney and said that she was going to delay the action another thirty days.

The husband made major adjustments with his employment, even taking a cut in pay. He had realized the significance of the statement, "For what is a man profited, if he shall gain the whole world, and lose his own soul [and his wife and daughter]? or what shall a man give in exchange for his soul?" (Matthew 16:26.) By the time the thirty days was up, the wife had decided not to sign the divorce papers.

THE POWER OF GOSPEL PRINCIPLES

Although their marriage nearly ended in divorce, the couple experienced something more important than their troubles as they began to center their lives on the Savior, his teachings, and his church. Their story illustrates a fundamental principle: gospel principles *will* help us deal with our differences, even the toughest, apparently unsolvable ones. Let me mention just a few of those principles.

There Were No Contentions

The Book of Mormon notes that after Jesus Christ appeared to the Nephites on the American continent, "the disciples of Jesus had formed a church of Christ in all the lands round about." (4 Nephi 1:1.) The gospel was taught as they had received it from the Savior, and in the thirty-sixth year "there were no contentions and disputations among them." (V. 2.) Verse thirteen notes that "there was no contention among all the people, in all the land." Even after a hundred years had passed away, "there was no contention in the land, because of the love of God which did dwell in the hearts of the people. And there were no envyings, nor strifes, nor tumults . . . ; and surely there could not be a happier people among all the people who had been created by the hand of God." (Vv. 15–16.) This condition apparently lasted more than two hundred years.

Could we suppose that during this period in Book of Mormon history, husbands and wives were living who theretofore had had differences in their marriages? What did Jesus and his disciples teach them that helped them learn to overcome or deal with the differences they had? Are these same principles taught and available for application for contemporary Latter-day Saints? Is it possible that we, too, might learn a process whereby we could live with "no contention or disputations" among us?

Patience

As discussed earlier, the first quality of love noted in 1 Corinthians 13:4 and Moroni 7:45 is long-suffering, or patience. The Old English equivalent of *suffer* is *allow*. When Jesus said, "Suffer little children . . . to come unto me" (Matthew 19:14), he simply meant "allow" them to come to me. Long-suffering therefore means long-allowing—permitting or tolerating certain things to happen. If this one principle alone were practiced by husbands and wives, many seemingly essential differences could become nonessential. One of the ten Cs is coexistence—learning to coexist or practice tolerance toward certain inconvenient conditions. We are learning to say, "I can live with it."

Other qualities of love noted in 1 Corinthians 13:4 and Moroni 7:45 also are helpful in dealing with differences in marriage. Couples who seek to develop the "pure love of Christ" (Moroni 7:47) become kinder (or more caring), envy one other less, become less arrogant, are not as easily angered or irritated, and gloat much less over each other's weaknesses or inadequacies. People developing Christlike love are learning to bear and endure more—in other words, to be more committed. All these qualities will greatly aid any married couple who is seriously trying to work out the differences that exist between them.

Reconciliation

When Jesus was on the earth during his mortal ministry, he taught his disciples to try to reconcile the differences that arose. Although not explicitly given to husbands and wives at the time, these instructions included every disciple who had a disagreement with another over differences.

Note that in this teaching on reconciliation, as well as in subsequent scriptures quoted in this chapter, the word *spouse* works as well as the word *brother:* "If thy brother [spouse] shall trespass against thee, go and tell him his fault between thee and him alone: if he shall hear thee, thou hast gained thy brother [spouse]." (Matthew 18:15.) Jesus suggested here that when someone has offended you, you have the obligation to go to him or her first, alone, and seek reconciliation. The observation that "if he shall hear thee" suggests that the person may not want to listen. Or perhaps the timing may be inappropriate. People often say that if they have been offended, the other person must come to them first. How many times in your life have you offended someone without knowing it? I suppose I have many times, but I'm sure I did not mean or want to offend anyone. That is one reason why you must start the reconciliation process. If you have been offended, sometimes the other person does not know how you feel.

Now, what if you have given an offense, and you know it. What should you do? Again, Jesus admonished, "If thou bring thy gift to the altar, and there rememberest that thy brother [spouse] hath ought against thee; leave there thy gift before the altar, and go thy way; first be reconciled to thy brother [spouse], and then come and offer thy gift." (Matthew 5:23–24.) If we are trying to do something religious or spiritual (that is, bringing a "gift to the altar") and know that we have offended someone, we should seek reconciliation before continuing. No matter whether we give or receive the offense, Jesus expects us to take the initiative for reconciliation. The verse also encourages us to do it soon or "quickly," before the situation gets out of hand or worsens. (See also 3 Nephi 12:25–26.) These simple teachings are of great value to Latter-day Saint couples who are trying to deal with their differences in a Christlike way.

Forgiveness

In addition to reconciliation, Jesus taught forgiveness, telling his followers that if they forgave others of their shortcomings, Heavenly Father would forgive them their weaknesses and in-adequacies. (See Matthew 6:12, 14–15.) The same concept of forgiveness was also taught on the American continent by the Savior after his resurrection. (See 3 Nephi 13:11, 14–15.) Our forgiveness of others usually signifies that we will not seek retri-bution against them for wrongdoing. The real benefit comes to the one doing the forgiving because the enormous sin of retaliation (or the desire for retaliation) is removed. Forgiveness is giving up the right to hurt someone who has hurt you. If husbands and wives lived the "eye for an eye and a tooth for a tooth" philosophy in marriage, we would, as Mohandas Gandhi observed, all soon be blind and toothless.

The commandment to forgive was given again in latter-day revelation even more forcefully when the Lord stated, "My disciples, in days of old, sought occasion against one another and forgave not one another in their hearts; and for this evil they were afflicted and sorely chastened. Wherefore, I say unto you, that ye ought to forgive one another; for he that forgiveth not his brother [spouse] his trespasses standeth condemned before the Lord; for there remaineth in him the greater sin. I, the Lord, will forgive whom I will forgive, but of you it is required to forgive all men." (D&C 64:8–10.)

Prayer

We are commanded twelve times in modern-day revelation to "pray always." Evidently, the Lord expects prayer to become a common practice among LDS husbands and wives. Why does the Lord tell us that we should "pray always"? That we may conquer Satan (see D&C 10:5), that we may be blessed with the Spirit (see 19:38), that we will not fall into temptation (see 20:33), that we will not lose our reward (see 31:12), that we may understand the scriptures (see 32:4), that we may be ready for the second coming of Christ (see 33:17) and abide, or survive, the day of his second coming (see 61:39), that we will not faint in doing the Lord's work and will have him with us in that work (see 75:11), that we may be blessed and do great good (see 81:3–4), that he will receive us unto himself (see 88:126), that all things will work together for our good (see 90:24), and that Satan will have no power over us (see 93:49).

Prayer can be a vastly underrated power in marriage for resolving differences. In one regional meeting, a general authority said that when couples come to him for marriage counseling, he always begins by asking one question, "Are you praying together?"

Almost always the answer is no. He then asks them to seek the Lord's guidance for one month for their marital concerns. He reported that when they return four weeks later, about half tell him that with the Lord's help, they have been able to resolve their differences and concerns.

There is another good reason why LDS couples should pray always. It is an excellent barometer of their marital relationship. Occasionally, when Susan and I have knelt down to pray and I have asked her if she would offer the prayer, she has hesitated and replied, "I'd rather not." She is so open and honest with her feelings that she finds it difficult to pray when we have allowed some unkind feelings or contention to arise. We have found that before either of us can pray, we first have to sit down, discuss our concerns, and resolve our feelings. This is in keeping with the biblical injunctions noted previously under "Reconciliation."

As a bishop I have had some powerful experiences with prayer. One night I just happened to drop by a home in my ward for a visit. As I walked in, I could feel the contention that was present. Several members of the family had been exchanging harsh words just before I arrived. I offered to leave, but the young wife asked me to stay. Before I said anything more, she asked if I would kneel down with the family and pray, which we did. We could feel the tension ease, and after we finished, they shared with me what had occurred before I arrived.

On another occasion I was visiting in a home with a couple who were having some major concerns. We talked for about an hour while I tried a number of counseling skills. But we were getting nowhere. Finally I suggested that we kneel down and each one of us say a prayer. The wife said that would be impossible since her husband didn't pray. We went ahead anyway, and after I prayed, the wife prayed. Then it was the husband's turn. He hesitated, then gave one of the most humble, thoughtful prayers I have ever heard. Praying together that night with the couple brought a spirit into the home that allowed us to constructively discuss their concerns, problems, and differences.

Temple Attendance

Early in the Restoration, the Saints were commanded to build temples, as the Lord said, "for the gathering together of my saints, that they may worship me." (D&C 115:8; see also 88:119–20.) We are encouraged to attend the temple for several reasons. Not only are we to enter and work in behalf of the deceased, but we are encouraged to go for our own benefit. Temples are to be places of thanksgiving and edifices where we can receive instruction. (See D&C 97:13.)

Elder Boyd K. Packer, in his book *The Holy Temple,* has noted: "The Lord said in the Old Testament, and again to the Prophet Joseph Smith (Psalm 46:10 and D&C 101:16), 'Be still, and know that I am God.' There is such a thing as learning to listen spiritually. There is such a thing as having pure intelligence poured into the mind. In the temple the meditation and contemplation that comes from a quietly observed reverence frequently results in such a pouring-in of intelligence and spiritual learning."[1] We are also encouraged to go to the temple when we have troubles and cares in our life. On this point, Elder Packer has written:

> When members of the Church are troubled or when crucial decisions weigh heavily upon their minds, it is a common thing for them to go to the temple. It is a good place to take our cares. In the temple we can receive spiritual perspective. There, during the time of the temple service, we are "out of the world."
>
> A large part of the value of these occasions is the fact that we are doing something for someone that they cannot do for themselves. As we perform the endowment for someone who is dead, somehow we feel a little less hesitant to pray fervently to the Lord to assist us. When young married couples have decisions to make, if they are near a temple there is great value in attending a session. There is something cleansing and clarifying about the spiritual atmosphere of the temple.
>
> Sometimes our minds are so beset with problems, and there are so many things clamoring for attention at once,

that we just cannot think clearly and see clearly. At the temple the dust of distraction seems to settle out, the fog and the haze seem to lift, and we can "see" things that we were not able to see before and find a way through our troubles that we had not previously known.[2]

When marital discord arises, going to the temple and partaking of the spirit there may put a couple in a frame of mind to mutually work on their concerns. The Lord is anxious to pour out knowledge on the Latter-day Saints (see D&C 121:33), and this outpouring often comes from insights and thoughts obtained while attending the temple.

Fellowship with the Saints

I firmly believe that marriage is strengthened when husband and wife meet and associate with couples who are committed to gospel values and ideals. We call each other "brother" or "sister." We worship together in sacrament meeting and symbolically "break bread," or eat together and renew our baptismal covenants to help and support each other. (See Mosiah 18:8–10.) These activities with our fellow believers builds up a supporting community that makes our lives richer and brings gospel blessings more fully into our lives.

There is also great value in attending classes where we can all teach one another. (See D&C 88:122.) By divine commandment, we are to watch over and care for each other. (See Ephesians 6:18; D&C 20:42, 47, 53; 88:123.) When we do these things and participate in home and visiting teaching, we help each other survive the hectic pace of life.

Paul eloquently described what happens when we join this unique community: "Now therefore ye are no more strangers and foreigners, but fellowcitizens with the saints, and of the household of God; and are built upon the foundation of the apostles and prophets, Jesus Christ himself being the chief corner stone; in whom all the building fitly framed together groweth unto an holy temple in the Lord: in whom ye also are builded together for an habitation of God through the Spirit." (Ephesians 2:19–22.)

The Sacrament and the Lord's Spirit

I also believe that a couple derive spiritual strength from partaking of the sacrament and receiving the attendant promise that they may always have his Spirit to be with them. (See D&C 20:77, 79.) I wonder, sometimes, if we really appreciate this blessing. When we allow the Lord's Spirit to be present in our homes, we are allowing ourselves to come under his influence. The Spirit softens our hearts, and we are better able to face and work through our differences as they arise.

In Galatians, Paul notes that the works of the flesh (or absence of the Spirit) promote hatred, variance, wrath, strife, and envy, among other things. Those who allow these conditions to permeate their homes "shall not inherit the kingdom of God." (5:19–21.) But those who do enjoy the fruits of spirit will have "love, joy, peace, longsuffering, gentleness, goodness, faith, meekness, temperance," and will not be desirous of vain glory, provoke one another, or be envious. (5:22–26.)

Scripture Reading

When discord or disharmony come into a marriage, perspective, strength, and insight for dealing with these problems can be gained by reading the scriptures. When we read them prayerfully and carefully, insights come both from the content of the word and the spirit of revelation. Of the scriptures, the Lord has noted, "These words [scriptures] are not of men nor of man, but of me; wherefore, you shall testify they are of me and not of man; for it is my voice which speaketh them unto you; for they are given by my Spirit unto you, and by my power you can read them one to another; . . . wherefore, you can testify that you have heard my voice, and know my words." (D&C 18:34–36.)

Shortly after Elder Ezra Taft Benson became President of the Church, he encouraged the Saints to read the scriptures. He particularly encouraged them to read the Book of Mormon, reiterating this wonderful promise given two decades earlier by Elder Marion G. Romney:

I feel certain that if, in our homes, parents will read from the Book of Mormon prayerfully and regularly, both by themselves and with their children, the spirit of that great book will come to permeate our homes and all who dwell therein. The spirit of reverence will increase; mutual respect and consideration for each other will grow. *The spirit of contention will depart.* Parents will counsel their children in greater love and wisdom. Children will be more responsive and submissive to that counsel. Righteousness will increase. Faith, hope, and charity — the pure love of Christ — will abound in our homes and lives, bringing in their wake peace, joy, and happiness.[3]

In the Book of Mormon itself, Nephi gave a similar profound promise that the words of Christ will help to give us direction in life: "Wherefore, I said unto you, feast upon the words of Christ; for behold, the words of Christ will tell you all things what ye should do. Wherefore, now after I have spoken these words, if ye cannot understand them it will be because ye ask not, neither do ye knock. . . . If ye will enter in by the way, and receive the Holy Ghost, it will show unto you all things what ye should do." (2 Nephi 32:3–5.)

When Latter-day Saint couples come to Jesus Christ and live the gospel fully, they will be able to draw on the spiritual resources he has provided to help them deal with their differences as they arise: "They were married, and given in marriage, and were blessed according to the multitude of the promises which the Lord had made unto them." (4 Nephi 1:11.) Perhaps we too, as did disciples of old, will reach a point where there can be "no contention in the land." (4 Nephi 1:15.)

PART 3

WAYS OF VIEWING DIFFERENCES IN MARRIAGE

13

NEW PERSPECTIVES
ON DIFFERENCES

As we conclude this book, *Dealing with Differences in Marriage,* let me help you gain a new perspective on the topic.

First, let's go back to the exercise in chapter seven on identifying differences. Just pause for a moment and review your list. Look at the ones that are of major concern for you. Read the following statement from B. H. Roberts over again: "In essentials let there be unity; in non-essentials, liberty; and in all things, charity!"

What are the essential and nonessential differences in your marriage? What are the ones that really matter? What are the ones that are merely annoyances or irritations with which you can simply coexist or exercise great patience?

Next, reread the 80/20 phenomena noted in chapter two on pages thirteen to fifteen. Think about what the 80 percent of your needs are that your spouse is meeting. Do you let your spouse know what needs are being met? Or are you focused on the 20 percent of your unmet needs? And while you are examining your 20 percent of unmet needs, remember that your spouse sometimes thinks about his or her unmet needs as well.

Finally, review the change-first principle in chapter eight. What changes could you make *first* in yourself that would make your marital relationship more satisfying for both of you? Read Matthew 7:3–5 again. What are your "beams"?

THE THINGS THAT UNITE US

Now we are ready for a new exercise. On another sheet of paper, or on the back of the exercise for identifying differences, write down the following statement on the top of the sheet: The things that unite us are greater than the things that divide us!

Make another list. Only this time write down all the things that unite you and your spouse. What brought you together? What holds you together? What areas or things of mutual concern and interest do you share? Go ahead and "count your many blessings."[1] Here are some things typically shared by LDS couples:

The restored gospel of Jesus Christ
Our testimonies of it
Our temple marriage
Our children
Our home or apartment
Places we have lived
Vacations
A specific crisis or difficulties we have overcome
Illnesses we have encountered and survived
A car, boat, or cabin
Our health
Our commitment to our marriage
Our employment and ability to earn a living
Our opportunity to continue learning and studying
The scriptures
Features of our personalities

Now, every time you decide to review and work on the exercise for identifying differences, *review and reread the above exercise first!* Always keep in mind the 80 percent of the relationship that is going well before you work on or become preoccupied with the 20 percent that needs attention. (Reread Philippians 4:8.)

There are also other ways you can *instantly* get a new perspective of your spouse, your marriage, and the differences you have. The petty but seemingly insignificant areas may instantly be viewed in a way that can change your whole outlook. Consider how you would view your differences if you were to receive either of these two slips of paper.

OPERATION DESERT STORM

The first piece of paper would be a telegram from the United States government ordering the husband or the wife into active military service. This occurred not long ago when the United States government entered Operation Desert Storm in Kuwait. Within one week in the BYU 33rd Ward where I was bishop during the fall of 1990, three young husbands serving in the army and national guard reserve forces each received a telegram calling them into active duty. Many of us shared the couple's concerns.

The sacrament service in which the three couples spoke before the men reported for duty was a memorable one. Every couple said the minor concerns that seemed to matter prior to the telegrams didn't seem to matter much now that the men were leaving. Faced with the separation and the uncertainty of the husbands' future, the couples viewed their marriages differently. Then, when the three young men returned home within the year, they also conveyed the feelings they had as they reported to the armories. One of the first things the husbands had to do was to fill out a will in case they did not return from the war.

Other husbands and wives report similar feelings when confronted with life-threatening situations. The day-to-day concerns seem to shrink in significance when the life of a husband, wife, or child is in jeopardy. So when you seem particularly challenged by your differences and you feel the need for a new perspective on what things are important in your marriage, think of the slip of paper, a simple telegram.

A LAB REPORT

The second piece of paper that could help you change your perspective on differences in marriage could be a laboratory report. Implicit in our marriage vows is the promise that we will abide with our spouses in sickness and in health, for rich or for poor, for better or for worse. During times of sickness, life-threatening situations often arise. It was so for an elderly LDS man in California.

I was in his stake to deliver a Know Your Religion speech.

After I finished, he came up with his walker and shared with me an event that had happened with him and his now-deceased wife. She had gone to the doctor one day, concerned about some growths on her cheek. The lab report informed them that she had cancer.

The aging husband described for me what their marriage was like as the cancer gradually began to eat away at her face. Because of the chemotherapy treatment, all her hair fell out. She had been a beautiful woman, but now she was ashamed of her appearance. The husband told me that little else mattered to him in the marriage from that point on except helping her through the difficult situation and an imminent death.

As the cancer progressed, she didn't want him or anyone else to see her. She just wanted to be alone. The husband told me, however, that as her condition grew worse, a light began to radiate from her face. He believed it was her spirit. The worse the cancer got, the brighter the light grew. He said he fell in love with the radiance about her face. He kept telling her how beautiful she was. At first she wouldn't believe him, but finally he convinced her of his love and concern. "She died," he said, holding back his tears, "believing she was the most beautiful woman on earth."

Perhaps you are concerned about shoes left on the floor, an untidy closet, an inability to communicate on a meaningful level, or some other difference on your list. Just think — what if either one of you got a cancer on the face and the disfigurement began. How many, if not all, of the "essentials" would quietly be transferred to the "nonessential" category.

President Kimball once noted the importance of standing by a spouse through difficult times. He said:

> While one is young and well and strong and beautiful or handsome and attractive, he or she can (for the moment) almost name the price and write the ticket; but the time comes when these temporary things have had their day; when wrinkles come and aching joints; when hair is thin

and bodies bulge; when nerves are frayed and tempers are taut; when wealth is dissipated. . . .

There comes a time when those who flattered us and those whose wit and charm deceived us may leave us to our fate. Those are times when we want friends, good friends, common friends, loved ones, tied with immortal bonds – people who will nurse our illnesses, tolerate our eccentricities, and love us with pure, undefiled affection. Then we need an unspoiled companion who will not count our wrinkles, remember our stupidities nor remember our weaknesses; then is when we need a loving companion with whom we have suffered and wept and prayed and worshipped; one with whom we have suffered sorrow and disappointments, one who loves us for what we are or intend to be rather than what we appear to be in our gilded shell.[2]

KALAUPAPA

January 14, 1991, was an unusual day for Susan and me. We were on a whirlwind tour of the Hawaiian Islands where I spoke to eight different church groups. We visited the islands of Hawaii, Maui, Molokai, Kauai, and Oahu . . . all in ten days.

We had a one-day break, however. I spoke in Molokai on Sunday, January 13, and was not scheduled to speak again until January 15 in Maui. So that meant we had January 14, a Monday, to do as we pleased. I was aware of Kalaupapa, a peninsula on the north side of Molokai, where people with leprosy had been isolated. When we were in Hawaii four years before, we had driven to the north side of Molokai, and from the cliffs overhead, we looked down 1,600 feet on the beautiful peninsula, which was about four miles square. From the distance we could see the aging buildings at Kalaupapa, still remaining today.

On this trip to Hawaii we decided to visit the community and made arrangements to take the one-and-a-half-hour mule ride down to Kalaupapa. Early Monday morning, we mounted our mules and began the trip down on the narrow, winding path.

We and twenty other members of the party arrived at the base camp in Kalaupapa, where a rickety old bus driven by one of the residents of Kalaupapa met us. During World War II, drugs were discovered that made leprosy noncontagious. The eighty-five residents of Kalaupapa were finally free to come and go as they chose, but the colony was home to most of them, and they chose to stay.

We boarded the bus and drove around on the few paved roads. Our tour guide gave an interesting brief history of the colony. We stopped at a small gift store and bought a book titled *Kalaupapa and the Legacy of Father Damien,* where we found more information about the Catholic priest, Father Damien de Veuster, his co-workers, Joseph Dutton and Mother Mairianne Cope, and others who devoted their ministries to serving the people with leprosy from the time that Kalaupapa was established in the early 1860s.[3]

About noon we rode the bus to the east side of Kalaupapa where we visited the recently remodeled chapel that had originally been built by Father Damien. While there, we learned that many married Hawaiian men and women contracted leprosy and were exiled to Kalaupapa. The remaining spouses had two choices: (1) they could accompany their spouses with leprosy to Kalaupapa and help take care of them. Those who chose to accompany their spouses were called "kokuas," or helpers. Or, (2) they could remain behind and let their spouses go to Kalaupapa to eventually die alone of the dreaded disease. Apparently many surviving spouses chose to go with their husbands or wives to Kalaupapa.

I was particularly interested in finding more about Jonathon Napela and his wife, Kitty, both of whom were Latter-day Saints. They arrived at Kalaupapa in 1873, after Kitty was diagnosed as having leprosy. Jonathon Napela was a magistrate on Maui, and the couple had children, but Brother Napela chose to go with his wife to Kalaupapa. He died of the disease six years later, in 1879. Kitty died of leprosy two years later, in 1881.[4]

After touring the facilities, we were offered a box lunch and given an hour to eat and relax. Susan and I went down to the seaside to eat. It is difficult to describe the beauty of the peninsula at Kalaupapa. At the risk of sounding commercial, it looks just like an advertisement out of a Hawaiian Airlines magazine. Nor is it possible to describe the feeling of isolation we had being there. After experiencing the remoteness of the location, we were better able to understand why leprosy was called the "disease of isolation." Once a family member got leprosy, they were sent to Kalaupapa never to see family members again. That included the many dozen children who arrived at Kalaupapa with the disease.

While we were eating our lunch, I turned to Susan and said, "Would you go with me to Kalaupapa?" She didn't know at first what I meant. "If I got leprosy and were sent here, would you come with me?" I asked. She didn't answer for a minute or so. Unknown to me at the time, I had asked her one of the most difficult questions of her life.

"What about the children?" she finally asked. I had not thought about that. "Yes," I replied after a while, "you would have to leave our children at home." All the fathers and mothers who came to Kalaupapa had to leave their children behind to be cared for by others.

Susan finally said, "Yes, I would go with you to Kalaupapa." I assured her that I too would accompany her as well.

Our tour ended, and we rode the mules back to the top of Molokai. We returned to our motel to prepare for the rest of the hectic tour. But before we retired to bed that night, we read a scripture, Ruth 1:16–17, that took on new significance for both of us: "Intreat me not to leave thee, or to return from following after thee: for whither thou goest, I will go; and where thou lodgest, I will lodge: thy people shall be my people, and thy God my God: where thou diest, will I die, and there will I be buried: the Lord do so to me, and more also, if ought but death part thee and me."

That moment of realization and recommitment has changed our marriage. Since that day with my wife at the beach at Kalaupapa, our marriage has not quite been the same. The differences we now have in our marriage just don't seem to matter as much anymore. The number of pillows we have on our bed, prolonged shopping trips to the mall with Susan, the fact that she doesn't put salt in tomato juice, our disagreement on what the right temperature ought to be, her ability to make the "minor" decisions, her belief that she can run to the grocery store and be back in ten minutes, our differences in how easy or hard we should be with the children, and her desire to throw away my army boots — somehow all those things now seem rather insignificant.

And maybe they all were insignificant — nonessential — even before we went to Kalaupapa.

CASE STUDIES

Now that you have become acquainted with some basic strategies for dealing with differences in marriage, let's gain some practice in applying them. You have differentiated between essential and nonessential differences, examined the change-first principle, and gone through the ten Cs of dealing with differences in marriage. That includes the foundation of *commitment, caring,* and *communication*. In addition are the frequent four: *coexistence, capitulation, compromise,* and *collaboration*. Added to these are the special cases of *confrontation* and *counseling*. Finally, and most important, is the impact of *Christ*. Let's see now if you and your spouse can go through the following twenty-five case studies and apply these principles. (Many of these case studies are also useful to discuss in classroom settings if you explain and teach the ten Cs to the participants.)

Read and consider each case study until you feel you understand the dynamics involved. Then try to arrive at a solution that might be mutually agreeable to the married couple in the case study. Assume all married couples in the studies are Latter-day Saints unless otherwise noted.

Case Study 1

Bill and Jan have a fifteen-year-old daughter, Becky, who turns sixteen on May 10. The junior class president, Jay, has asked Becky for a date to the high school junior prom on April 5. Jan thinks Becky should not date until she turns sixteen. Bill feels that their daughter should be allowed to go because she has not dated up until now and has complied with the "spirit of the law." How might this difference be resolved using the ten Cs?

Case Study 2

Using the scenario in case study 1, consider this additional information: Jay, the young man wanting to date Becky, is not a Latter-day Saint. His father is the boss where Bill works and is the one who hired Bill. Under these conditions, should Jay be allowed to take Becky to the prom? How might this difference be resolved using the ten Cs?

Case Study 3

Scott and Jennie are active Latter-day Saints, the only members in their neighborhood. Their ten-year-old daughter, Lisa, has made many friends in the area, and her best friend, who is not a Latter-day Saint, has invited her to a birthday party. The party, however, is on Sunday afternoon and will be held at a local skating rink. Scott thinks Lisa should be allowed to go. Jennie feels strongly that she should not go because that would not be keeping the Sabbath day holy. How might this difference be resolved using the ten Cs?

Case Study 4

Dave and Teresa live in the same LDS community as Teresa's parents. Long before Dave and Teresa were married, Teresa's parents established the tradition of inviting all their married children and grandchildren over to their house each Sunday evening for a family home evening. Everyone usually attends. Teresa wants to participate in this family tradition and drive the short distance each week to visit her parents. Dave thinks that once a week is too much and informs Teresa he would rather just go to her parents house occasionally. How might this difference in marriage be resolved using the ten Cs?

Case Study 5

Jason and Nancy have been married just three months. Jason grew up with a group of friends who discussed sex openly. Many of his friends boasted of their supposed sexual encounters, though Jason never took part in the boasting and, in fact, kept himself chaste. Nancy grew up in a fairly conservative environment where sexual matters were never discussed. Both Jason and Nancy complied with the law of chastity and were worthy to marry in the temple. Now that they are married, however, Jason expects to have sexual relationships several times a week. Nancy doesn't want to keep a count and prefers sexual intimacy a few times a month when both are spontaneously aroused. How might they resolve this difference in their marriage using the ten Cs?

Case Study 6

Jay and Alice have been married fifteen years, and they find themselves financially hard-pressed. While Jay is preparing his income tax, he asks Alice to sign some invoices stating that they both were at a certain business convention during the previous year. Jay wants to deduct the expenses from his income tax. The only problem is, they never went on the trip. Alice believes it is both immoral and illegal to falsify income tax records and indicates these feelings to her husband. He replies that it is all right and tells how a friend falsified some similar records the previous year to obtain a larger tax return. Jay wants her to sign the papers. Even though they desperately need the money, Alice doesn't think it is right. How might they resolve this difference in their marriage using the ten Cs?

Case Study 7

Tom has an annoying habit of leaving his dirty dishes on the table when he fixes some food or a snack. Up until now, Jane has picked up his dishes and put them in the sink for him. But Jane is getting tired of this and asks Tom to please put his own dishes in the sink. He replies that he is too busy and besides, Jane is home all day. Tom thinks that cleaning up is part of her job. How might this difference be resolved using the ten Cs?

Case Study 8

Ron and Kristi have been married for eight years and have two children, both of whom are now in school. Kristi feels that she would like to go back to work half-time at her former place of employment. The only problem is that she would have to work in the afternoon and would not be home until five. Ron thinks she shouldn't work because he wants Kristi at home when their two children arrive from school. They talk it over. Kristi still wants to take the job. Ron wants her to be at home when the children arrive from school. He also adds that since he presides in the home and holds the priesthood, he should make the decision. How might this difference be resolved using the ten Cs?

Case Study 9

JoAnn's best friend is getting married on July 14, and JoAnn wants to go. Doug, her husband, has his high school reunion the same day in another city, and he wants JoAnn to attend his reunion with him. How might this difference be resolved using the ten Cs?

Case Study 10

Mike, who joined the Church a little over a year ago, has recently married Geri in the temple. Mike's parents, who are not Latter-day Saints, are coming for a visit for two days. Mike's father is a chain smoker, and they anticipate that he will want to smoke in their home once they arrive. Geri is adamantly against allowing him to do so. Mike feels that Geri should have greater tolerance with his father's smoking habit so that his father won't be offended. How might this difference be resolved using the ten Cs?

Case Study 11

In the above situation, Mike's mother also drinks coffee. Geri is opposed to letting her drink coffee in their house and refuses to serve it. Again, Mike asks Geri to be more tolerant of his parents. How might this difference be resolved using the ten Cs?

Case Study 12

Bob and Gail have argued many times about money. As long as Bob can remember, he has had a temper. Now that he is married to Gail, he continues to have temper tantrums whenever they disagree about money. Bob yells a lot and sometimes throws things around the house during such discussions. Although he has never struck Gail, he sometimes restrains her and won't let her go while they are "talking." Gail doesn't want to talk about money matters when Bob acts this way. He, however, sees no problem in his behavior and wants to talk it out no matter how he acts. How might this difference be resolved using the ten Cs?

Case Study 13

Ben and Leslie, both returned missionaries, plan to marry in two months. He wants them to have a child right away. Leslie, however, wants to wait at least one year before they have a child so she can finish her bachelor's degree at the university. Both feel strongly about their positions. How might this difference be resolved using the ten Cs?

Case Study 14

Ted and Barbara plan to buy a new car. They have agreed on everything, including the make and model. However, they prefer different colors. Ted is adamant that the new car be red. Barbara is equally firm that their new car be white. How might this difference be resolved using the ten Cs.?

Case Study 15

Carl and Lauri have six hundred dollars from their income tax refund. Carl wants to take the money and buy a new monitor and some other equipment for their home computer. Lauri would like the money to purchase some new furniture for their house. How might this difference be resolved using the ten Cs?

Case Study 16

Sid has enrolled their nine-year-old son, Ryan, in a junior league baseball team and pushes him to excel. Ryan is not very athletic and feels he is a disappointment to both his father and his teammates. He informs his parents that he wants to quit. His mother, Beverly, agrees and feels he should quit since the pressure concerning baseball is causing so much contention in the home. Sid wants Ryan to continue. How might this difference be resolved using the ten Cs?

Case Study 17

Paul and Jill have been married for eight years, but their marriage is becoming more and more difficult for both. Several times they have sat down to try to work through their problems, but nothing seems to work. Jill loves Paul and wants to stay with him, but her frustrations continue to grow. She has thought seriously about divorce. She asked Paul to go with her to see the bishop, but he refused. Two months later, after they had a major confrontation, she asked him to go with her to see a marriage counselor. Again he refused, saying he thought they could work out their problems on their own. Jill feels, however, that there is little hope for their marriage unless they get some outside help. How might this difference be resolved using the ten Cs?

Case Study 18

Rita is a successful business executive. Her recent promotion requires her to travel more than Scott, her husband, would like. They do not have children. At least once a month now, Rita must fly to other cities for two or three days at a time, in company with Brad and Jim, two other business executives who are also Latter-day Saints. Scott is uneasy about her traveling with the men so often. Rita doesn't understand his anxiety since she feels that she is loyal and dedicated to him and their temple marriage. She loves both her husband and her work and asks Scott to trust her on the trips. How might this difference be resolved using the ten Cs?

Case Study 19

Before Eric and Sandra were married, Eric had many male friends and enjoyed their company. Now that he has been married to Sandra for a year, his friends continue to stop by unannounced.

Eric frequently invites them to stay not only for a meal, but overnight, and they sleep on the couch. Sandra feels that his friends are taking advantage of his generosity and her cooking. Last week two different friends of Eric came on two different nights. Eric invited both to eat and sleep overnight. Sandra thinks that his friends come too often. How might this difference be resolved using the ten Cs?

Case Study 20

Dale has a slight lisp that annoys Janice, his wife, especially when he calls her "Thweetie" ("Sweetie"). She doesn't know if she should be flattered by his term of endearment or ask him not to say it. How might this difference be resolved using the ten Cs?

Case Study 21

Tom has just been offered a good job in Boston, Massachusetts, a position he has sought for a long time that carries with it a substantial salary increase. Janet, his wife, prefers not to move from their home in California, because her aging mother is very ill. Janet would like to stay in California and be able to attend to the needs of her mother. Besides, she also likes living in California and doesn't want to take their three children out of their schools. Janet feels that Tom's present job and salary are adequate for their needs. How might this difference be resolved using the ten Cs?

Case Study 22

Larry and Amy are deeply in love and have been married ten years. They have one major concern. Larry has recently begun snoring, and Amy is a light sleeper. His snoring has become so disruptive that Amy seldom sleeps more than a few hours each night and awakes exhausted each day. She wants to sleep in another room. Larry wants her to stay and sleep by him. How might this difference be resolved using the ten Cs?

Case Study 23

Enid finds out that a year ago Wally, her second husband, had sexually abused her fourteen-year-old daughter by Enid's first marriage. Wally says that he has not touched her since and that at the time he swore to himself to never repeat it. Enid loves Wally and wants to stay with him, but she is concerned about her daughter. Wally is a good provider and seems to treat Enid well. But she is afraid that he might abuse her daughter again. How might this difference be resolved using the ten Cs?

Case Study 24

Keith insists they should pay a generous fast offering of thirty dollars a month. Debbie thinks they should pay only ten dollars. They have two children and earn an average income. How might this difference be resolved using the ten Cs?

Case Study 25

Betty believes that Harry should be in charge of all religious activities in the home since he holds the priesthood and, as she says, "is the head of the home." She feels it is his duty in regard to family home evening, family prayers, and scripture reading. Harry feels that Betty should share with him the responsibility of doing these things and asks for her assistance. She refuses on the grounds that when she helps in directing these religious activities, he backs off and leaves it all up to her. How might they resolve this difference using the ten Cs?

NOTES

CHAPTER 1

1. Brent A. Barlow, *Just for Newlyweds* (Salt Lake City: Deseret Book Company, 1992), 4–9.
2. Claude Richards, "J. Golden Kimball: The Story of a Unique Personality" (Salt Lake City: Bookcraft, 1966), 99–100.
3. Edward L. Kimball, ed., *The Teachings of Spencer W. Kimball* (Salt Lake City: Bookcraft, 1982), 314; italics added.

CHAPTER 2

1. David R. Mace published two books in 1982 that elaborated on these ideas: *Love and Anger in Marriage* (Grand Rapids, Michigan: Zondervan) and *Close Companions: The Marriage Enrichment Handbook* (New York: Continuum). In the latter book he devoted chapter ten to "Love, Anger, and Intimacy," pages 90–99, and chapter eleven to "Settling Disagreements by Negotiation," pages 100–107.
2. Brent A. Barlow, "The Temper Trap," in *Twelve Traps in Today's Marriage and How to Avoid Them* (Salt Lake City: Deseret Book Company, 1986), 121–34.
3. "Celestial Marriage," *The Seer,* vol. 1, no. 6 (June 1853): 90.
4. B. H. Roberts, *A Comprehensive History of The Church of Jesus Christ of Latter-day Saints* (Provo: Brigham Young University Press, 1965), 1:131.
5. See Barlow, *Just for Newlyweds,* 4–9.
6. Frank D. Cox, *Human Intimacy: Marriage, the Family and Its Meaning,* 5th ed. (Saint Paul, Minnesota: West Publishing Company, 1987), 160–61.
7. James Dobson, *Love for a Lifetime* (Portland, Oregon: Multnomah, 1987), 59.
8. Ibid., 65.

CHAPTER 3

1. See Arthur J. Norton and Jeanne E. Moorman, "Current Trends in Marriage and Divorce among American Women," *Journal of Marriage and the Family* 49 (February 1987): 3–14.
2. Kimball, *Teachings,* 314–15.

3. Spencer W. Kimball, "The Privilege of Holding the Priesthood," in *Priesthood* (Salt Lake City: Deseret Book Company, 1981), 4–5.

4. Kimball, *Teachings,* 314; italics added.

5. Ezra Taft Benson, *Teachings of Ezra Taft Benson* (Salt Lake City: Bookcraft, 1988), 532–33; italics added.

6. Rodney Turner, *Woman and the Priesthood* (Salt Lake City: Deseret Book Company, 1972), 264–65.

7. Gordon B. Hinckley, "What God Hath Joined Together," *Ensign,* May 1991, 74.

8. Ibid., 72.

9. Spencer W. Kimball, *Marriage* (Salt Lake City: Deseret Book Company, 1978), 46–47.

10. See Leslie Cameron-Bandler, *Solutions: Practical and Effective Antidotes for Sexual and Relationship Problems* (San Rafael, California: FuturePace, 1985), 115–28.

11. Diane Medved, *The Case against Divorce* (New York: Donald I. Fine, 1989), 12.

12. Kimball, *Marriage,* 37–38.

13. Dean L. Larsen, "Marriage and the Patriarchal Order," *Ensign,* September 1982, 13.

CHAPTER 4

1. See Michael Popkin, *Active Parenting* (San Francisco: Harper & Row, 1987), 36, for the Family Constellation Chart, which describes characteristics of the first, only, second, middle, and youngest child. See also Rudolph Dreikurs, "The Child's Position in the Family," in *Children — the Challenge* (New York: Hawthorne Books, Inc., 1964), 20–35; and Walter Toman, *Family Constellations* (New York: Springer Publishing Company, 1976).

2. See Paul Popenoe, "Are Women Really Different?" *Family Life,* February 1971, 1–2.

3. Joyce Brothers, *What Every Woman Should Know about Men* (New York: Simon and Schuster, 1981), 11.

4. See ibid., 13.

5. See ibid., 36.

6. Ibid., 39–40.

7. See Joe Tanenbaum, *Male and Female Realities: Understanding the Opposite Sex* (San Marcos, California: Robert Erdmann Publishing, 1990), 48.

8. Anne Moir and David Jessel, *Brain Sex: The Real Difference between Men and Women* (New York: Dell Publishing, 1989), 5.

9. Christine Gorman, "Sizing Up the Sexes," *Time,* 20 January 1992, 42–51.

10. See ibid., 45.

11. Deborah Tannen, *You Just Don't Understand: Women and Men in Conversation* (New York: Ballantine Books, 1990), 18.

12. See Sidney M. Jourard, *The Transparent Self* (Princeton: D. Van Nostrand Company, Inc., 1964), 46–55.

13. See Brent A. Barlow, "Notes on Mormon Interfaith Marriages," *Family Coordinator,* April 1977.

14. Kimball, *Teachings,* 314.

15. Ibid., 315; italics added.

CHAPTER 5

1. See Helen Singer Kaplan, *The New Sex Therapy: Active Treatment of Sexual Dysfunctions* (New York: Brunner-Mazel Publishers, 1974), 5–33.

2. See Desmond Morris, *Intimate Behaviour* (New York: Random House, 1971), 71–78.

3. Tanenbaum, 49.

4. See ibid., 49–50.

5. See Moir and Jessel, 103–4.

6. See ibid., 107.

7. See ibid., 109.

8. Ibid., 133.

9. Ibid., 111–12; italics added.

10. William Masters and Virginia Johnson, *Human Sexual Inadequacy* (New York: Little, Brown and Company, 1970), 87.

11. Ibid., 335.

12. See James Leslie McCary, "Sexual Myths and Fallacies," in *Human Sexuality* (New York: D. Van Nostrand Company, 1973), 477–83.

13. Brent A. Barlow, "They Twain Shall Be One: Thoughts on Intimacy in Marriage," *Ensign,* September 1986, 49–53.

14. *Webster's New World Dictionary,* 1979, 434.

15. Ibid., 469.

16. See Brent A. Barlow, *What Husbands Expect of Wives* (Salt Lake City: Deseret Book Company, 1983), 60–65.

17. Kimball, *Teachings,* 312.

18. Val D. MacMurray, "The Sexually Well Person," in "Sexual and Emotional Intimacy: A Need to Emphasize Principles," *Journal of Association of Mormon Counselors and Psychotherapists* 8, no. 1 (January 1982): 18–19.

19. Roy Welker, *Preparation for Marriage* (Independence, Missouri: LDS Department of Education, Press of Zion's Printing and Publishing Company, 1942), 93–94; italics added.

CHAPTER 7

1. See Chuck and Barb Snyder, *Incompatibility: Grounds for a Great Marriage* (Sisters, Oregon: Questar Publishers, Inc, 1988), 15–33.

2. Kimball, *Teachings,* 305.

3. As quoted by B. H. Roberts, in General Conference Report, October 1912, 30.

CHAPTER 8

1. A condensed version of this chapter appeared in the *Ensign*, September 1992, 14–17, as "To Build a Better Marriage."
2. Melvyn Kinder and Connell Cowan, *Husbands and Wives: The Guide for Men and Women Who Want to Stay Married* (New York, Signet Books, 1990), 37–38; for additional information on the change-first principle, see Richard B. Stuart, *Helping Couples Change: A Social Learning Approach to Marital Therapy* (New York: The Guilford Press, 1980), 202.
3. "Recollections of the Prophet Joseph Smith," *Juvenile Instructor* 27, no. 10 (May 15, 1892): 302.
4. Ibid., no. 15 (August 1, 1892): 472.
5. Susa Young Gates and Leah D. Widtsoe, *The Life Story of Brigham Young* (New York: The Macmillan Company, 1931), 251.
6. Joseph Fielding Smith, comp., *Scriptural Teachings of the Prophet Joseph Smith* (Salt Lake City: Deseret Book Company, 1993), 355.
7. Kinder and Cowan, 73.
8. Smith, *Scriptural Teachings,* 355.

CHAPTER 9

1. These books, all published by Deseret Book Company, are *What Wives Expect of Husbands* (1982), *What Husbands Expect of Wives* (1983); *Twelve Traps in Today's Marriage* (1986), and *Just for Newlyweds* (1992).

CHAPTER 10

1. For example, see David R. Mace, "Settling Disagreements by Negotiation," chapter 11, in *Close Companions: The Marriage Enrichment Handbook* (New York: Continuum Printing Company, 1982); and Carlfred Broderick, "Negotiating a Joint Script," chapter 4, *Couples* (New York: Simon and Schuster, 1979).
2. *Webster's New World Dictionary*, 1979, 95.
3. Kimball, *Teachings*, 307.
4. *Webster's,* 102.
5. Ibid., 96.
6. For in-depth discussions of the win-win relationship, see Dennis Waitley, *The Double Win* (New York: Berkley Publishers, 1986); Steven R. Covey, "Think Win/Win," chapter four, in *Seven Habits of Highly Effective People* (New York: Simon and Schuster, 1989), 204–34.

CHAPTER 11

1. *Webster's,* 104.
2. James Dobson, *Love Must Be Tough: New Hope for Families in Crisis* (Waco, Texas: Word Books, 1983), 8.

3. See ibid., 8–9.
4. Ibid., 76.
5. *Webster's*, 113.

CHAPTER 12

1. Boyd K. Packer, *The Holy Temple* (Salt Lake City: Bookcraft, 1980), 79.
2. Ibid., 180–81.
3. Marion G. Romney, as quoted by Ezra Taft Benson, "Cleansing the Inner Vessel," *Ensign,* May 1986, 6; italics added.

CHAPTER 13

1. *Hymns* (1985), no. 241.
2. Kimball, *Teachings,* 310.
3. See Anwei V. Skinsnes Law and Richard A. Wisniewski, *Kalaupapa and the Legacy of Father Damien* (Honolulu: Pacific Basin Enterprises, 1988).
4. See Joseph H. Spurrier, *Great Are the Promises unto the Isles of the Sea* (Salt Lake City: Hawkes Publishing, Inc, 1978), 23; see also Spurrier, "Jonathon Napela: Quiet Hero of Hawaii," *Ensign,* August 1978, 49–51; Donna J. Bowen, "Love Story Hidden in Graves of Lepers," *Church News,* 25 June 1988, 11–12.

INDEX

Adultery, commandment against, 50–51

Affection, without natural, 48

Analogy: of perch and sparrow to differences in marriage, 6; of "Fish and Fowl" to differences in marriage, 7, 37; of "mote and beam" to change-first principle, 76; of broken grandfather clock to a marriage in crisis, 117

Anecdotes: seminar at Aspen Grove Camp, 3–5; marriage seminar with David and Vera Mace, 8–10; anger between Joseph and Emma Smith, 11–12; 80/20 phenomena, 13–15; parental marriage models, 27–28; shopping techniques, 57–58; pillows, 58–59; tourist activities, 59–60; food and drink, 60–61; energy levels, 61–62; temperature reactions, 62–63; religion, 63–64; making decisions, 64; parenting, 64–65; perception of time and space, 65–66; throwers and savers, 66; coexistence and untidy roommate, 97–98; imaginary scale and commitment, 99–100; example of martyrdom vs. capitulation, 100–101; example of compromise, 102–3; two examples of collaboration, 104–5; example of planning a wedding, 105–7; example of a "book thief" and confrontation, 110–11; an errant young executive, 121–23; author's experiences with prayer, 127; perspective changed through Operation Desert Storm, 137; perspective changed through cancer, 137–38; the leper colony at Kalaupapa, 139–42

Anger between married couples, 9–11, 13

Appreciation in falling in love, 21

Aspen Grove Camp, seminar at, 3–5

Attraction in falling in love, 20–21

Benson, Ezra Taft, 130

Cameron-Bandler, Leslie, 20–23

Cancer, anecdote about spouse dying of, 137–39

Capitulation (fifth of ten Cs): 98–100, 110

Caring (second of ten Cs), 89–90

Case studies: dating before sixteen, 143–44; dating non-LDS, 144; attending Sunday afternoon non-LDS party, 144; attending in-laws' weekly family nights, 144; compromising on sexual intimacy, 145; falsifying income tax records, 145; cleaning up after oneself, 145; mother working half-time, 146; attending wedding or high school reunion, 146; allowing non-LDS in-laws to smoke and drink coffee in

157

your home, 146; giving in to temper tantrums to solve money problems, 146–47; starting a family or finishing school first, 147; deciding color of a new car, 147; deciding on use of income tax refund, 147; resolving contention over children's activities, 147–48; resolving serious marital crisis, 148; resolving difficulties of wife's work schedule, 148; accommodating premarital friendships, 149; resolving petty annoyances, 149; moving family to accept a new job, 149; resolving disturbing annoyances, 149; dealing with child sexual abuse, 150; paying a reasonable fast offering, 150; sharing responsibility of religious training, 150

Change, individual, four areas of, 80–84

Change-first principle: and responsibility, 75; and analogy of "mote and beam," 76; in day-to-day behaviors, 77; and law of the harvest, 77–78; and law of the boomerang, 78–79; and four areas of individual change, 80–84; review of, 135

Christ (tenth of ten Cs): as "Counsellor," 120; errant young executive and, 121–23; power of gospel principles and, 123–26; and appearance to the Nephites, 123; on patience, 124; on reconciliation, 124–25; on forgiveness, 125–26; on prayer, 126–31; on temple attendance and prayer during marital discord, 128–29; as cornerstone of the household of God, 129; spirit of, and the sacrament, 130; on scripture reading, 130–31. See also Jesus Christ

Clothes, picking up, 102–3

Coexistence (fourth of ten Cs), 96–98, 110

Collaboration (seventh of ten Cs), 103–5, 110

Commitment (first of ten Cs), 19–20, 85–86; to third entity, 87–90

Communication (third of ten Cs): importance of, 6; nature of, 90–91; when to use, 91–92, 95; where to use, 92–93, 95; why we use, 93–95; three-question quiz on observation and, 93–94

Compatibility, 14–15

Compromise (sixth of ten Cs), 28, 101–3, 110

Conflict, relationship of, to differences, disagreements, and anger, 9–10, 13

Confrontation (eighth of ten Cs): definition of, 108; and examples of core symbols, 109–10; and example of a "book thief," 110–11; three-step process of, 111–14

Contentions and gospel principles, 123–24

Core symbols of marriage, 109

Counseling (ninth of ten Cs): definition of, 114; who to go to for, 114–16; and LDS Social Services, 116–17; professional, 117–19; horizontal and vertical, 120

Courtship and compatibility, 14–15

Cowan, Connell, 76–77, 84

Damien, Father, 140

Decisions, anecdote about making, 64

Desert Storm, anecdote about couples affected by, 137

Development, spiritual, and anger, 11

Differences between male and female: physical, 28–32; cultural and genetic, 30; mental, 30–33; and capabilities of the brain, 30–33; and processing of information, 32–33; and use of language, 32–33; and sexual response, 42–45; biological, with regard to sexuality, 43–45; that cause divorce, 52

Disagreements, relationship of, to differences, conflict, and anger, 9–10, 13

Disappointment/disillusionment, 22

Divorce: contemplation of, 4; statistics and trends of, 6, 10, 12, 16, 19; and newlyweds, 12; epidemic of, 16–17; as an escape, 17; justification of, 17–18; causes of, 18–20; pathway to, 20–23; is process of three phases, 20; major differences that cause, 52

Dobson, James, 14–15, 110–11, 113

Education, collaborating to obtain, 104–5

80/20 phenomena, 13–15, 50, 97, 135–136

Energy levels, anecdote about, 61–62

Environment, social, influences of parent and, on child, 26–27

Equality of sexes, myth of, 32

Excitement as first stage of sexual response, 39–40

Executive, anecdote of young, 121–23

Expectation as a stage in the ending of love, 21–22

Family-of-origin differences, 27–28

Fellowship, importance of, 129

"Fish and fowl" analogy, 7, 38

Food and drink, anecdote about, 60–61

Forgiveness, 11–12, 125–26

Fulfillment: of needs, 13–15; LDS philosophy of sexuality and, 50–51

Gandhi, Mohandas, 126

Golden Rule. See Law of the boomerang

Gospel. See Principles, gospel

Grandchildren, relationship to, 36

Grandfather clock: buying, 105; analogy to, 117

Gratitude for sexuality, 53–55

Habituation in falling in love, 21

Hinckley, Gordon B., 18

Intimacy, physical, twelve stages of, 40–42

Jesus Christ: and Sermon on the Mount, 76, 78; and law of the harvest, 78; and law of the boomerang, 78–79; as third entity to commitment in marriage, 87–88. See also Christ (tenth of ten Cs)

Johnson, Virginia, 39–40, 49

Kalaupapa, anecdote about, 139–42

Kimball, J. Golden, 6

Kimball, Spencer W.: analogy of "Fish and Fowl," 7, 37; on celestial marriage, 7; on marriage and divorce, 16–17, 19; on happiness in marriage, 23; on differing natures of men and women, 37–38; on major differences causing divorce, 52; on adjustments in marriage, 71; on capitulation, 98–99; on standing by one's spouse, 138–39

Kindner, Melvyn, 76–77, 84

Language, use of, by genders, 32–33

Larsen, Dean L., 24

Last days, signs of, 19, 47–48

Law of the boomerang, 78–79

Law of the harvest, 77–78

Love: three stages of how, begins, 20–21; five stages of how, ends, 21–23

Mace, David R. and Vera, 8–10

MacMurray, Val, 53–55

Marriage: toleration of differences in, 3–5; author's observations on successful, 4; surviving, 5; model of conflict-free, 6; sacrifice and selflessness in, 17; Satan's influence on, 19; of convenience, 19; working at, 23–24; example of parental models in, 27–28; and compromise, 28; and sexual normality, 45–49; essential

differences in, 72–73;
nonessential differences in, 73–
74; core symbols of, 109. *See also*
Case studies; Ten Cs of marriage
Masters, William, 39–40, 49
Media's influence on sexual
perceptions, 47–48
McCary, James, 49–50
Medved, Diane, 23
Menopause and sexuality, 49
"Mote and beam" analogy, 76
Myths, sexual, 49–50

Napela, Jonathon and Kitty, 140
Natures, complementary, of men
and women, 37–38
Needs of married couples, meeting,
13–15
Nephites and appearance of Jesus
Christ, 123
Newlyweds and dealing with
differences, 12

Oneness vs. sameness, 6, 11
Operation Desert Storm, anecdote
about couples affected by, 137
Orgasm: as third stage of sexual
response, 40; statistics of
experiencing, 43–44

Packer, Boyd K., 128–29
Parenting, anecdote about, 64–65
Party, martyr roles in, 100–101
Patience and gospel principles, 124
Perception: dwelling on, or beliefs,
21; reorientation of, in the
ending of love, 22–23
Perch and sparrow analogy, 6
Pillows, anecdote about, 58–59
Plateau as second stage of sexual
response, 40
Pratt, Orson, 11
Prayer, 126–27
Pretense for appearance's sake, 18
Principles, gospel: lack of
contentions, 123–24; patience,
124; reconciliation, 124–25;
forgiveness, 125–26; prayer, 126–
27; temple attendance, 128–29;
fellowship, 129; sacrament, 230;
scripture reading, 130–31

Reconciliation, 124–25
Relationship and commitment, 22
Reproduction, 52–53
Resolution as fourth stage of sexual
response, 40
Response, sexual: four stages of, 39–
40; importance of twelve stages
of physical intimacy to, 42;
differences in, 42–45; and
gratification, 44
Roberts, B. H., 72, 89, 135
Romney, Marion G., 130–31
Roommate, anecdote about untidy,
97–98

Sacrament and the Lord's Spirit,
130
Sacrifice in marriage, 17
Satan, influence of, on contemporary
marriages, 19
Savers, anecdote about throwers
and, 66
Savior. *See* Christ (tenth of ten Cs);
Jesus Christ
Scale, using imaginary, 99–100
Scripture reading, encouragement
of, 130–31
Selfishness, sexual, 50–52
Selflessness in marriage, 17
Sex: normalcy of, in marriage, 45–
49; influence of media on attitudes
about, 47–48; myths concerning,
49–50; and selfishness of sharing,
50–52; God's commandment
relating to, 52–56; in marriage is
divinely sanctioned, 52–53; and
well being, 53–55; normal
functioning of, 55–56. *See also*
Response, sexual
Sharing, sexual, three elements of,
52
Shopping, differences in attitudes
on, 57–58
Sibling order, 27
Signs of the times, 19, 48
Smith, Joseph, 11–12, 81–82, 84
Snyder, Chuck and Barb, 69–71
Space, anecdote about perception
of, 65–66
Spiritual: anger and, development,

11; guidance known as vertical help, 120

Stinginess, sexual, 51–52

Temperature reactions, anecdote about, 62–63
Temple attendance, 128–29
Ten Cs of marriage: commitment, 85–89; caring, 89–90; communication, 90–95; coexistence, 96–98; capitulation, 98–101; compromise, 101–3; collaboration, 103–5; confrontation, 108–14; counseling, 114–19; Christ, 120–31.
Testosterone, 44
"Thief," book, anecdote of, 110–11
Threshold as a stage in the ending of love, 22
Throwers, anecdote about, and savers, 66
Time, anecdote about perception of, 65

Tithing, anecdote about, 63–64
Tolerance and coexistence, 96–98
Tourist activities, anecdote about, 59–60
Turner, Rodney, 18

Verification as a stage in the ending of love, 23
Vindication as a stage of verification, 23

Weakness, personal, shown through prayer, 79
Wedding, differences in planning, 105–7
Welker, Roy, 55–56
Whitmer, David, 11–12
Word of Wisdom: physical, 80; mental, 81–82; social, 82; spiritual, and change-first principle, 83
Works of the flesh, 130

Young, Brigham, 81–82